Social Media, Sexuality, and Sexual Health Advocacy in Kolkata, India

A Working Report

Social Media, Sexuality, and Sexual Health Advocacy in Kolkata, India

A Working Report

Dr Rohit K Dasgupta
Loughborough University

Mr Pawan Dhall
Varta Trust

Research team:

Dr Rohit K Dasgupta
Loughborough University

Mr Pawan Dhall
Varta Trust

Dr Paul Boyce
University of Sussex

B L O O M S B U R Y
NEW DELHI • LONDON • OXFORD • NEW YORK • SYDNEY

First published, 2017

BLOOMSBURY PUBLISHING INDIA PVT. LTD.
New Delhi London Oxford New York Sydney

ISBN: 978-93-86432-65-0

10 9 8 7 6 5 4 3 2 1

Published by Bloomsbury Publishing India Pvt. Ltd.
DDA Complex LSC, Building No. 4, 2nd Floor
Pocket 6 & 7, Sector C
Vasant Kunj, New Delhi 110070

Typeset by Fortune Graphics, Ring Road, Naraina, New Delhi

Printed at Anvi Composers, Paschim Vihar, New Delhi

CONTENTS

ACKNOWLEDGEMENTS

The authors would like to thank the various funding bodies which made this research and the subsequent report publication possible. We would like to firstly thank the Wellcome Trust which made funding available under its small grants scheme to undertake this project. In addition, the Winchester Centre for Global Futures, University of Southampton made a further grant to help us with the publication. We would like to thank the various organisations and individuals that we worked with in Kolkata for taking part in the discussions through our formal focus groups and interviews but also the informal discussions. We thank the Varta Trust for providing institutional support in Kolkata and the Institute for Media and Creative Industries at Loughborough University for making available time for us to undertake this project and the subsequent writing up. We are particularly thankful to Dr Paul Boyce who was part of the research team but ultimately could not participate in the writing up of this report. We are grateful to Mr Kaustav Bakshi and Prof. Paromita Chakrabarti of Jadavpur University for hosting our international symposium and the speakers and audience who were receptive to our ideas and findings from this study. Rohit would also like to thank Dr Sharif Mowlabocus for his support and mentorship and inviting him as a researcher on the 'Reaching Out Online' project which became the genesis and inspiration for this one. Several individuals – Dr Ani Dutta, Dr Debanuj Dasgupta, Mr

Tim Aldcroft, Dr Sangeeta Datta and Ms Rittika Dasgupta – have provided various forms of help during our time in Kolkata. Finally thanks to Bloomsbury India for agreeing to publish this book.

INTRODUCTION

On 01 July 2015, the official 'Digital India' campaign was launched by the Prime Minister of India, Narendra Modi. The initiative aimed to create a strong digital infrastructure to deliver services more efficiently through digital mediums and encourage digital literacy. All three initiatives are key areas for development and this project addresses two of these key components- delivering sexual health services through social media and developing digital literacy for successful online peer outreach. '*Mobile-ising for Sexual Health: Social Media, Sexuality, and Advocacy*' is a Wellcome Trust funded scoping project that was undertaken in collaboration between the University of Southampton (later Loughborough University) and University of Sussex in the UK and the Varta Trust in Kolkata, India.

The Principal Investigator and funding award holder is Dr Rohit K Dasgupta of Loughborough University. The project team also consisted of Dr Paul Boyce, University of Sussex and Mr Pawan Dhall, who was Consultant and project partner from the Varta Trust.

The project ran between May – October, 2016 with focus groups taking place between May–August, 2016 with analysis and writing up this report taking place between October 2016-January, 2017. The primary aims of this project were to:

1. Engage with outreach workers, health promotion experts and service users of sexual health organisations in Kolkata

working with gay and other men who have sex with men and trans* women to map if there are existing digital resource driven services and if they can be mobilised further.

2. Map out the digital literacy skills that might be required by health workers to navigate mobile and digital platforms
3. Build a critical understanding of how digital and mobile media can be deployed for sexual health advocacy within the gay, men who have sex with men and trans* community.

CHAPTER 1

SEXUALITY, AND DIGITAL QUEER INDIA

Kolkata, Scene One

Rohit and Paul arrived in Kolkata on a humid August morning in 2016 to begin research for the present project. As soon as the plane touched down, an announcement was made that people could turn on their mobile phones. A series of beeps were heard as people called their family and friends to inform they have landed. As Rohit and Paul walked to the baggage counter, they were informed that data charges on roaming would cost £6/MB, a princely sum but a friendly passenger advised that Kolkata airport now had free Wi-Fi. It took 5 tries to log in to the network. As Rohit and Paul walked out to get a pre-booked taxi, the queue felt thinner than in previous years. Most people seemed to be typing away furiously on their phones. Once outside we noticed a steady stream of cars with Uber and Ola brands advertised on their windshields waiting for their customers. Digital India seemed to have reached West Bengal.

Kolkata, Scene Two

As the taxi snaked its way out of the airport hundreds of BJP (Bharatiya Janata Party) flags became visible. These are the flags of the newly ruling right wing government in India. They were surprising as the ruling party of India has yet to gain a stronghold in West Bengal but we are informed this is for an impending party conference. A few minutes later on VIP Road we are greeted by faces of Mamata Banerjee, the Chief Minister of West Bengal who has been returned to power in 2016 with an even larger majority on the promise of economic progress and 'free Wi-Fi' across the city (something yet to be implemented). It is strange to see the complete disappearance and obliteration of the familiar hammer and sickle of the Communist Party of India (Marxist), which ruled the state for 34 years.

The celebrated Delhi High Court judgment of 2009 in Naz Foundation v. Union of NCT of Delhi represents a crucial moment in the queer history of India. The judgement read down Section 377 of the Indian Penal Code, a Victorian remnant which has been used expressly to regulate sexual conduct and criminalise non-reproductive/non-heterosexual sex (also see Bhaskaran, 2002 and 2004). As Arondekar (2009) argued, in the colonial period, the law was employed to control 'criminal' populations such as hijras and certain tribes whilst in contemporary India the law exists to continue exerting control over sexual and gender minorities. The 2009 Naz judgment marked the end of a decade long (or even longer) struggle by various groups to try and argue for decriminalisation of sexual minorities. One of the primary arguments employed by Naz and other groups was the detrimental effect Section 377 was having on rolling out sexual health prevention programs. They particularly called out the government's stance towards homosexuality and the problem it caused in tackling the growing HIV/AIDS epidemic amongst 'men who have sex with men' in India. They argued that the presence of this law prevented such men from accessing sexual healthcare for fear of legal persecution – this being a strategy that was on the cusp of linking sexual rights and HIV prevention as symbiotically imperative. The 2009 judgment represented the outcome of long-term activism, and a liberal marker for social attitudes toward gender and sexual difference and diversity in India. It was even more concerning then, that after the progressive verdict from the High Court, and four years of legal challenges from other pressure groups (religious and political), a shock Supreme Court judgement threw all the hard earned social and legal recognition back to turmoil.

On 11th December 2013; the Indian Supreme Court, in a shock judgement, reinstated Section 377, effectively re-criminalising sexual acts 'against the order of nature' (this being the technical wording of the legal code). This ruling which displaced the Delhi High Court's earlier ruling reinstated what was a colonial law back into the social and cultural fabric of the country.

This battle around Section 377 has had a long and twisted history even before the Supreme Court announced its verdict. On 04 July, 2011; a mere two years since the reading down of Section 377, Ghulam Nabi Azad, the then Health Minister of India went live on television denouncing homosexuality.

At an HIV/AIDS conference in New Delhi, Mr Azad described same-sex sexual activity as 'unnatural' and asserted that it was imported from the West. His views were widely condemned by international organisations such as the UNAIDS as well as large sections of the media and human rights activists. After several weeks of pressure and protest action, Azad finally relented issuing an apology, claiming that his words were taken out of context. However, as the video of his statement, which is widely available online testifies, this is false. He later claimed that he wanted to state that HIV and AIDS were unnatural and not being gay. His half-hearted apology and insensitive comments towards queer people were widely condemned. Given his portfolio as Health Minister at that time, such comments were bound to have an impact on sexual health testing and safer sex advocacy campaigns.

It would be useful to point out here that the online queer networks made sure that this video was available to all viewers, through its dissemination over both online listservs and forums. It also helped to developed a critical response from the community towards the Minister and his comments. Through new media, the public were being informed about the ideological policies of the Minister of Health and by extension critiquing institutions of governance and the very legitimacy of having a seemingly homophobic health minister (also see Bachcheta, 1999, 2007; Banerjea, 2014). First-hand accounts and incriminating images such as those made by Azad can now be captured and communicated almost instantly via digital technologies and thereby contributing to 'processes of protest diffusion and the mass mobilisation of civil societies' (Cottle and Lester, 2011: 8). Cottle and Lester further argue that in such ways 'local and global communications can impenetrate, conditioning each other and intensifying political pressures for change'.

The government in India has been divided over the issue of decriminalising homosexuality in India. When Voices Against 377, a Delhi based coalition of human rights groups filed an intervention in support of the original petition by Naz in 2001, the Home Ministry submitted a defence of Section 377 whilst the Health Ministry supported a 'reading down' in the later stages of the proceedings. Following the historic judgement by the Delhi High Court which decriminalised homosexuality, various private individuals (mostly from faith based religious organisations) and a government panel was set up to review the judgement.

> We declare that Section 377 IPC, insofar it criminalises consensual sexual acts of adults in private, is violative of Articles 21, 14 and 15 of the Constitution.[1]

The government panel composed of P. Chidambaram, the Home Minister and Ghulam Nabi Azad, the Health Minister amongst others. The panel decided to not participate in an appeal and let the Supreme Court determine the 'correctness' of the High Court ruling, prompting many to see this as tacit governmental approval[2]

---

[1] *Naz Foundation v. Government of NCT of Delhi and Others*, 2 July 2009, WP(C)7455/2001, p. 105, section 132

[2] The International Gay and Lesbian Human Rights Commission (IGLHRC) reported that 'Indian activists are praising this decision as a symbol of tacit support for decriminalization in this landmark case'.

(Waites, 2010: 977). However, the IGLHRC cautioned that leaving the decision to the Supreme Court was unpredictable as it might be 'unwilling to intervene in moral issues'.

The IGLHRC caution came true when the Supreme Court decided to reinstate Section 377. In fact, during the proceedings, Justice Mukhopadhyay in response to Mr Anand Grover, one of those who pointed out the societal repercussions that Section 377 has; in it leading homosexuals to be seen as degraded and perverse by the society; he argued that it was the social reformer's job to change society and not the Court's.[3]

The judgement by the Supreme Court sent shockwaves across the country and the wider world. There was surprise that the Supreme Court of a democratic (perceivably liberal) country like India would have such a blatant disregard for the dignity and rights of sexual minorities in the country. The retrogressive nature of the judgement did not just impede the progress of sexual minority rights in India alone but across the world especially those in the global South who had taken strength from the Indian story to challenge laws and social norms in their own countries.

Queer India is also Digital India which is made and re-made through LGBTQ activism and desires (Dasgupta, 2015; Dave, 2012). Queer people in India as other parts of the world are creating spaces and 'communities' using digital and social media and navigate their daily existence through their everyday interaction and presence on these sites. Queer online spaces in India can be mapped as a vast terrain of digital sites that range from gay blogs (Gajjala and Mitra, 2008), to listservs created specifically for queer people (Roy, 2003) to social networking sites such as Planet Romeo and more generic social networking spaces such as Facebook. Since 2010 with the proliferation of smart phones and mobile technology, queer locative applications such as Grindr have also become popular, especially in the metropolitan cities such as Bangalore, Delhi, Mumbai

[3] This is available from *Notes of Proceedings in Suresh Kumar Kaushal* v. *Naz Foundation*, February 23 to March 27, 2012; Supreme Court of India; p. 76.

and Kolkata, for those who can afford such hardware and data connection. Queer cyberspace allows public sites on the internet to be co-opted; doubling up as a public space to form 'community' and a private space for intimate encounters. Queer space is thus not about claiming territory but rather identifying new possibilities out of the existing space (see Dhall, 2016). Media representations of queer people in India have changed at different periods of time. Whilst some sections of the media have been sympathetic to queer people, other sections of the media, fuelled by jingoistic nationalism, have castigated and portrayed queer people in a very negative light (see Vanita and Kidwai, 2000; Vanita, 2002; Shrivastava, 2005). These have been major factors and a driving force behind the emergence of an alternative social space offered by the internet.

The contemporary moment (2009 onwards) has seen the emergence of a more public queer articulation and consciousness in India. Whilst the queer subject in India has largely been formed around the law incorporating the queer male citizen within the discourse of rights based politics, it would be wrong to think of the queer male in India through only a discourse on legal rights. Gupta (2005) provides a brief history of Indian queer spaces through the mid 1990's. He notes that during the 1990's organisations such as Good As You (GAY) in Bangalore, Humsafar Trust in Mumbai, Humraahi in Delhi and Counsel Club in Kolkata were formed which began holding weekly/monthly support and social meetings for gay and queer identified men. These meetings, as Gupta further elaborates, focused on diverse issues such as being gay, the social compulsion to marry, family and so on. Over time this moved to issues around sexual health practice and HIV/AIDS. As a final point we should mention, the growth of queer organising and communities in India is also directly related to international sexual health funding that helped queer male communities converge and form under NGO's and charities (see Boyce, 2006, 2007, 2014).

CHAPTER 2

SEXUAL HEALTH AND MEN WHO HAVE SEX WITH MEN / TRANS* OUTREACH IN KOLKATA

The timeline for sexual health outreach among men who have sex with men and trans* women in Kolkata (and West Bengal) can be retraced to at least the early 1990's, and it more or less coincides with the emergence of the HIV epidemic as well as the beginnings of a politically organized queer movement in India – different from the much older traditional hijra and kothi community structures or mobilizations (Counsel Club, 2002). Work with men who have sex with men and trans* people has often been brought together in sexual health promotion and HIV prevention in India, as in other countries. For the most part this has arisen from circumstances where effeminately identified and performing subjects, who might otherwise be normatively judged as male bodied, had often been brought into the HIV prevention risk group category 'men who have sex with men.' Subsequent activism has effected at least a partial change in such circumstances, whereby especially trans* subjects have created more distinct spaces for recognition within health promotion practice, media, and legal frameworks in India. In terms of sexual health work with people identified as sexual and gender minorities, however, male-to-male and transgender subjects and subjectivities nonetheless share some common historical trajectories. In tracing some of these commonalities here in respect of the development of community-based sexual health outreach work in Kolkata we seek to foreground the value of looking back as a means to better comprehend the present.

In particular we want to indicate ways in which the early years of HIV prevention and sexual health work, in India as elsewhere, were characterised by a period of transition, from what we typify as analogue health promotion work toward strategies embedded in social media and the rapid and social wide up-take mobile technologies in India. Transitions in modes of communication have been intimately intertwined with transitions in ways in which sexualities and genders have been experienced, globally. India offers an instructive example in this regard as the period of the mid 1990s onward witnessed a rapid neo-liberal expansion of the economy, which in turn engendered significant and salient changes in family life, individual aspirations and emerging possibilities for new and contemporary ways of thinking about and experiencing non-heteronormative genders and sexualities. Such personal and social changes were closely linked to the emergence of HIV as a global epidemic. In India especially sexual and gender minority peoples' activism around their health needs helped to catalyse a rights based movement that has gone on to transform recognition of sexual and gender diversity in state and society over the last three decades – often in contested and not always in linearly progressive terms. We offer a specific perspective on such transitions in this section, as a means to ground our project in a deeper perspective on Kolkata as a contextual example. The story of sexual health work with men who have sex with men and people of transgender experience in Kolkata sheds insight into such problems and processes. This in turn sheds light on changing experiences and engagements in sexual life-worlds over time, not only for purposes of health promotion but in terms of sites and self-understandings regarding sexual practice and subjectivity.

The period since the 1990's saw significant changes in communication technologies in India and beyond when India opened up its markets and made its first foray into the global economy (see Dasgupta, 2017). The early days of HIV prevention outreach work in Kolkata took place at a time when there was little or nothing in the way of digital media as an attribute of people's day-to-day lives in the city – people in India did not commonly have cell phones at this time and internet connectivity was sparse. Much community-based organizing in this era (for any purpose) necessarily entailed an analogue dynamic. By this we mean ways of acting and being in the world that were not characterised by digital communication technologies. For the purposes of HIV prevention and sexual health interventions such ways of interacting involved an emphasis on meeting people in social contexts – as geographically dispersed throughout any given city or other locale. This was a common model of outreach work with so-called gender and sexual minority peoples at the time – globally. Such work involves engaging people in socio-sexual spaces such as cruising areas, bars (also see Mowlabocus et al., 2015). Safer sex promotion messages, condom distribution, and sexual health awareness work occurred in such contexts as a face-to-face activity, a strategy that persists in the present day, but which in the early 1990's was necessarily the only mode of operation available, much as socio-sexual contacts could also mostly only be mediated in person.

Early HIV prevention work in Kolkata, and as in many other settings, involved initiatives to map and document socio-sexual contexts in the city. The aim of such work was to generate demographic, geographic and epidemiological information in a manner that might point to 'hot spots' in the city where health workers might target and meet what were so-called sexual and gender minority persons. The model was to propound and extend separate health promotion models – aimed at distinct populations. While highly valuable in terms of stressing community-based approaches to sexual health and HIV prevention a consequence has been to portray HIV and sexual health issues as most associated with particular population groups, such as men who have sex with men, trans women, sex workers. Notwithstanding special risks and vulnerabilities faced by such populations, and the positive effects of community mobilisation in these terms, as a means of health promotion mobilisation surveillance and outreach models predicated on epidemiological separateness continue to confound realisation that heterosexually practicing peoples are found to be most at risk of HIV transmission in many parts of the world. HIV and sexual health work globally has tended to tread a complex and somewhat indeterminate path in these terms – between a positive focus on risk populations and an enduring paucity of perspective on such peoples as a part of the general populations.

Where media was involved in most global environments sexual work in the 1990s this involved print publications for the most part. Kolkata provides an instructive context in which to reflect back on such circumstances. One of the key publications for men who have sex with men and people of transgender experience in the early 1990's was the magazine Pravartak. Printed in small print runs, Pravartak was affiliated to the sexual and gender minority support group Counsel Club. Pravartak was available in one or two commercial outlets in the city as well as being available through subscription, via which it would be sent out to people in Kolkata, further afield in West Bengal, and in some instances beyond.

As a device for community connectivity for people of non-heteronormative experience Parvartak played a role similar to other magazines found in India at the time (like *Bombay Dost* etc). The magazine also acted as a vital conduit for communication, whereby address details for correspondence were published enabling exchanges of letters between those seeking support and advice about their experiences of sexual and/or gender difference. One of the most profoundly affecting aspects of the research for the present publication involved looking back at some of the letters sent to Pravartak and Counsel Club over the years from 1992 onwards. These have been informally archived by Pawan Dhall and the Varta Trust.

Paul too recalls coming to live and working in Kolkata in the mid 1990s (on HIV prevention work for men who have sex with men). The social work revolving around Counsel Club and Pravartak were vital elements for Paul, as a stranger in the city seeking to come to know the non-heteronormative socio-sexual world that may be available. It was a mode of being that required leg-work, going out to meet people, hanging out in cruising areas (not just for sex, or for health promotions work but for sociality too). Socio-sexual intimacy was only available via such means. In turn such modalities of intimacy might be seen to have effected sexuality's affective contours and possibilities. Where mutual contact with other same-sex desiring and transgender experiencing peoples could only be achieved in specific spaces, and over time ways for thinking of and experiencing onself as same-sex desiring and or gender or sexuality different take shape in isomorphic correspondence with the ways in which the world one lives in make possibilities for living, experiencing self in such terms become available. This is the central tenet of the intimacy and globalization theses, for example, which emerged in sociology of the 1990s, relating transformations intimacy to political-economic changes. Such transformation have included new possibilities for individualistic aspiration and ways of being, as connections to family and more broadly socially determined ways of being have seen to be altered as an outcome of altered modalities of living and working.

Changes in the possibilities for sexual subjectivities and intimacies have been strongly associated with such changes. The Global Gay thesis, for example, has been strongly advocated in association with such transformation, where newly emerging and transformative possibilities for gay (and by association LGBTI) were connected to the effects of globalising political economies, new social transformation, new possibilities for communication and travel – all of which have made gay self-identification emerge as way of being. Critiques of this position point to associated complexities of terms and identities such as gay. India has offered an especially instructive example here. Early days of HIV prevention, for example, quickly bifurcated along the lines of those who promoted outreach and sexual health initiatives aimed at gay men and those who argued that such a focus missed out the cultural particularities of the India context, where much same sex sexual activities, and non-heteronormative ways of being, cold not be captured under rubrics such as gay.

Earlier, in 1994, Naz Foundation International (NFI), an INGO based in London, started work on sexual health among MSM and trans* women in India. In Kolkata, they started the Naz Calcutta Project, which later grew into an NGO called Praajak (in 1997-98). NFI and Praajak brought in an emphasis on 'MSM' as terminology, arguing that sexual behaviours and not sexual identities should be the focus in safeguarding sexual health in the Indian context. And yet, the term MSM itself was co-opted by the community as a 'sexual identity' – often as an indigenous expression in rejection of 'western labels' like 'gay' but feeding into the very identity discourse it was supposed to question.

They also argued that sexuality was expressed along gendered lines in India rather than in terms of sexual orientation and that the much larger population of kothis was 'more authentic' and deserved greater attention than numerically fewer and 'culturally disconnected' gay and bisexual identified men. This lead to the formation of CBOs focussed largely on kothis like Pratyay Gender Trust, Prantik Bongaon, Bandhan and PLUS Kolkata in and around Kolkata all through the rest of 1990s and early 2000s. But it has also been argued that the kothi construct was 'created' as an outcome of globalized power play (not the least by donors), which either looks at queer expressions everywhere through a homogenizing (LGBT) lens or compensates for this simplification with another simplistic approach of emphasizing the 'indigenous as authentic'. Such an approach overlooks complex ground level realities (where identities and vulnerabilities are not conveniently correlated or compartmentalized), and feeds into inadequate policy and programme emphases (Reddy, 2005).

Counsel Club counter-argued that numerical strength should not be a marker for HIV interventions; that sexual health was meaningless without an emphasis on sexual identity and human rights, and groups like Counsel Club were not limited to a handful of gay and bisexual men, and that too just in Kolkata. In 1999-2000, Counsel Club experimented with branches in places like Siliguri, Durgapur, Barasat and Midnapore in response to growing membership from these places. Gradually, the discourse shifted to the fact that kothis and panthis did not constitute the larger mass of MSM or trans* women in India – many members of these populations did not even identify with these terms, let alone gay or bisexual (Joseph and Dhall, 2000).

The HIV epidemic is often cited as the prime catalyst behind queer community mobilization in India, but other viewpoints stress that HIV is only one element in sexual health and it was only one among several concerns that motivated and energized the early queer support forums (Das and Dhall, 2013). Nonetheless HIV was an important point of engagement as can be seen from a review of the literature related to regional support and community groups in West Bengal such as Counsel Club and its affiliated magazine Pravartak – these being among the earliest politically inspired queer support forums in Kolkata (and India). The July-December 1994 issue of Pravartak carried a report titled 'Towards Reality – A Report by the Pravartak Representative to the West Bengal Sexual Health Project'. In the same issue, the safer sex column carried an article titled 'Condoms, Not Culture'. While STI/HIV prevention information received most emphasis, emotional and psycho-social support around gender and sexuality diversity were also recognized as key aspects of sexual health, and increasingly as a matter of right.

The HIV epidemic also provided a breakthrough in terms of breaking the silence around a public discourse on sex and sexuality in India, and lead to large-scale resource mobilization through international donor support as well as Indian government policy and funding support for HIV interventions. This helped queer support forums strengthen their organizational base, particularly those of men who have sex with men, and trans* women (Das and Dhall, 2013). Early government interventions were largely unknown to the larger public and had little connection to the communities it purported to work with. But a more serious start was made with quasi-governmental initiatives like the West Bengal Sexual Health Project (WBSHP) in 1994, which was a collaboration between the state government, National AIDS Control Organisation (NACO)[4] and the then Overseas Development Agency of UK (now the Department for International Development – DfID) (Kumar, 1998). Among the very first such initiatives in India, WBSHP was instrumental in mobilizing a wide range of civil society, government and donor agencies, and took the first steps in developing a plan for a state-level HIV response – as a model for state level intervention that might be replicated elsewhere in India. It undertook civil society capacity building and organized key sexual health conferences, contributing to the discourse around and eventual establishment of targeted interventions as the centre point of the HIV response in the state and India. This approach of 'targeting' already marginalized communities had its detractors (in that it had the potential to further stigmatize them as 'vectors' of HIV infection), but WBSHP was also among the first initiatives in India that promoted community participation and ownership of the HIV response through CBOs, prominent among which was Durbar Mahila Samanwaya Committee, a pioneering collective of female (and later male and transgender) sex workers, which has gone on to become internationally well-recognised.

---

[4] National AIDS Control Organisation is the apex policy making, funding and capacity building agency that leads the HIV response in India.

At this early stage the participation of MSM and trans* women communities was limited and activists had to struggle hard to be vocal and visible in sexual health forums and the media, and till the next decade or so there were no government-supported targeted interventions to serve these communities. This was probably a reflection of inherent lack of understanding about gender and sexuality among key stakeholders, denial, and homophobia/transphobia, which also resulted in targeted intervention approaches suitable for brothel-based female sex workers being considered as default models for all other vulnerable communities. WBSHP continued till about 2002, by which time most states in the country, including West Bengal (in 1998-99), had set up State AIDS Control Societies, which were linked to NACO at the Centre in terms of policy guidelines, capacity building and facilitating flow of funds to NGOs and CBOs.

In 1999, Counsel Club, sister NGO Integration Society and lesbian and bisexual women's support group Sappho co-organized the 2nd Network East conference in Kolkata (an eastern India networking event for sexual minorities).[5] Among the key speakers at the conference was Trilochan Singh, the then Project Director of West Bengal State AIDS Prevention & Control Society (WBSAPCS). He agreed to the need for sexual health interventions for LGBT communities, but remained non-committal in terms of actual support. It was not till 2002 that WBSAPCS provided funding support to any MSM/trans* women's CBO in the state – this was a small fund of ₹40,000 provided to Integration Society to organize the 3rd Network East Conference in Kolkata (Palm Avenue Integration Society, 2002).

The 'identity/rights' versus 'health services' debate between

[5] Title sheet of the conference report read: 'Network East '99: Showing the Way to a Sustainable Networking Programme for Sexual Minorities in Eastern India – An Initiative of Counsel Club and Sappho and Supported by Palm Avenue Integration Society, Calcutta'. A dedication line read: 'Dedicated to the courage of Mamata-Monalisa and NP-Mou and in service of all sexual minorities – for their mental and physical well-being'.

CBOs and NGOs in West Bengal was more or less settled by the early 2000s[6], when the two sides (primarily Integration Society and Praajak) agreed that these issues had strong convergence. Both agencies conducted key sexual health operations research and needs assessments in the period 1998-2000 and efforts were made to develop a three-way collaboration with WBSAPCS for a large scale HIV intervention in 2001. Eventually nothing came of these efforts – government officials tried to hide the lack of political will to recognize the existence of MSM and trans* women, and instead put the blame on intra-community disputes. This was notwithstanding the fact that in 1999 Kolkata had already witnessed what was possibly South Asia's first rainbow pride walk, which received widespread media coverage.

The studies conducted by Integration Society and Praajak were among a number of similar studies facilitated by WBSHP since 1996-97, the first being a needs assessment conducted by Praajak in and around Kolkata. In 2002, Integration Society participated in a behaviour surveillance study commissioned by NACO through ORG-MARG in key metropolitan cities (NACO, 2002). But, as mentioned earlier, these studies never lead to a concerted, large-scale government-aided intervention programme. This contributed significantly to research-fatigue and distrust among the communities concerned, and it was not till 2003-04 when yet another needs assessment lead to an actual intervention for the first time.

When this happened, it was a feat because most CBOs of MSM/trans* women and NGOs working with these populations in West Bengal came together to form MANAS Bangla, a state-wide network, which was granted one of the largest targeted interventions in India (Joseph, 2005). Credit should also be given to the top leadership in WBSAPCS, which for the first time was openly supportive, albeit the fact that they too 'played safe' by not granting

[6] Email correspondence between queer and health activists in response to the article *MSM Networks: Identity Categories Versus Identity Continuum* by Deep Purkayastha in Pukaar, October 1999.

the intervention to any one agency and insisted that MANAS Bangla as a network be provided funds. Community morale at this time was particularly also combative because of an insensitive move by WBSAPCS to make it mandatory for MANAS Bangla to 'provide 100 individuals' for an annual HIV sentinel surveillance (HSS) or risk losing the intervention grant in the making. This was successfully resisted on the grounds that nowhere did government policy state that intervention applicants needed to first participate in an HSS; nor was it ethical or respectful of human rights to 'force' individuals in a surveillance even if it was promised to be unlinked, anonymous. This was evidence of the negotiation power of coalitions, as MANAS Bangla successfully negotiated an agreement that it would participate in the HSS only after one year of intervention implementation, training of its workforce and confidence building measures with the communities concerned, which had long awaited meaningful action to respond to the HIV epidemic.

MANAS Bangla's HIV intervention started with many firsts and advantages. With CBOs across the state participating in the network (including in the often neglected northern part of the state), the intervention led to large-scale community mobilization with about 8,000 individuals being line listed (registered) and brought into the services net. NACO at this stage was keen on population size estimations, and MANAS Bangla's coverage provided an insight into how vast the MSM and trans* women populations could be. The intervention also provided a significant boost to community visibility, and most importantly led to a broadening of understanding that MSM and trans* women were not limited to traditional hot spots (cruising areas in parks, transport points and near toilets), and that there were many more outreach avenues yet to be tapped. Festivals like Jagaddhatri Puja in Chandannagar, community fairs, and places with holy shrines like in Ghutiari Sharief, to the south of Kolkata in South 24 Parganas district were covered for the first time; as also massage parlours and khols (residences of individuals that functioned like open houses for sexual networking within circles more or less known to the owner) (Singh et al., 2012).

But gradually, over the next half a decade or so (2004-10) the disadvantages were also evident. In the beginning, most constituent member CBOs were organizationally in nascent stages and the network itself acquired an unwieldy structure in terms of administration. A few CBOs of MSM and trans* women were unhappy about being excluded; other civil society groups were critical that the sexual health concerns of lesbian, bisexual women and trans* men had been ignored. A narrow focus on 'high-risk' MSM, thanks to the restricted thinking in NACP, led to further criticism and disillusionment in the community.

The initial strength of the network began to dissipate as WBSAPCS pressured its civil society partners into prioritizing health services provision, with only a token and reactive response to human rights violations and need for legal aid by community members (SAATHII, 2011). This development was particularly sad as the network's original aim was not to just implement a medicalized HIV intervention at the cost of broader sexual and mental health and community development issues involved. At this stage HIV interventions across India faced a situation when their outreach workforce was pressured into achieving unrealistic outreach targets, which led to a compromise on quality service provision. Capacity building measures continued to lag behind requirements; stigma and discrimination in health care and legal or police settings remained far from eliminated, though MANAS Bangla did make sensitization inroads in these areas and established linkages with friendly service providers. HIV care, support and treatment concerns of MSM and trans* women were not addressed adequately and instances of biased treatment or treatment denial continued to be reported.

Since 2002, NGOs like Solidarity and Action Against The HIV Infection in India (SAATHII) have made an entry into the HIV response in West Bengal and other parts of India. SAATHII focussed on addressing the capacity building gaps in the HIV response rather than service provision. In West Bengal, SAATHII implemented a number of large scale capacity building programmes focussed on organizational development, knowledge building on gender, sexuality, SRH, HIV and human rights, skills building in HIV prevention, care, support and treatment, counselling, documentation and advocacy. While SAATHII largely aligned its programmes to the national HIV response, it combined an element of social justice with public health priorities, advocating a stand that did not reduce issues like sexual health and HIV only to medical interventions.

In a programme funded by the DFID Civil Society Challenge Fund, it facilitated the creation of civil society capacity building and advocacy coalitions, one each in Odisha and West Bengal, which brought together a range of 62 civil society agencies involved in SRH and HIV interventions representing 60,000 gender and sexual minorities, PLHIV and other vulnerable groups like children and youth over a period of five years 2008-13. Its major achievements were in the areas of organizational development and resources generation (including mainstreaming SRH, gender and sexuality into organizational policies of NGOs and CBOs), sensitizing and developing linkages between CSOs and health care providers and legal service providers, supporting a number of PLHIV facing stigma and discrimination in obtaining justice through litigation or alternate redress mechanisms, and media advocacy (Hazra et al., 2012).

Another important outcome of SAATHII's coalition based interventions was that it helped prepare a number of CBOs of MSM and trans* women in West Bengal for implementing Project Pehchan (2010-15). This was an ambitious 18-state community systems strengthening and SRH service provision programme funded by the Global Fund to Fight AIDS, Tuberculosis and Malaria and implemented by a civil society consortium lead by India HIV/AIDS Alliance. In West Bengal SAATHII acted as a Sub-Recipient of the grant and worked with 38 CBOs (nationally the number of CBOs involved was 200). Till date it remains their largest single-country programme on HIV for sexual minorities.

Pehchan aimed to supplement the national and state HIV responses by helping increase population coverage and broaden the traditional basket of HIV services provided by traditional HIV interventions (Hazra and Ghosh, 2016). It aimed to bring in a number of mental health, anti-violence/legal protection and social security services because these were believed to have an impact on HIV vulnerability. Unfortunately, till date there is no evidence that NACP has absorbed any of the lessons learnt from Pehchan. The programme's refreshing approach to address the health concerns of the hitherto neglected sections of MSM populations (that is, beyond so-called 'high risk' kothi sub-groups, and in particular the panthis, male sexual partners of kothis believed to mostly play the penetrative role in anal/oral/inter-femural sex) was dropped midway in favour of the traditional approach. In West Bengal, as in many other states, few of the CBOs strengthened and supported by Pehchan, in many cases in districts not covered earlier, have been brought into the NACO/SACS fold.

Stepping back in time again, during the third phase of NACP (2007-12), a key development was the differentiation between trans* women and MSM populations – an acknowledgement that the two populations had specific concerns beyond certain common ones. There was vigorous debate for exclusive trans* women interventions, and the Pehchan programme and NACO concretized this process. Consequently, the Integrated Biological and Behavioural Surveillance conducted by NACO has started reporting separate data on STI/HIV prevalence for MSM and trans* women, with a clear indication that HIV prevalence among trans* women is markedly higher (NACO, 2016).

Looking at the last five years of the history of sexual health interventions in West Bengal, the scenario is mixed. Around the time Pehchan started, West Bengal had several interventions implemented by both MANAS Bangla and individuals CBOs operational. But there were shortcomings, including criticism that these interventions did not reach out to enough trans* women, especially hijras, and that they were biased towards MSM. But paradoxically, they were also not believed to cover diverse sections of MSM, other than kothis, who, in spite of being 'classified' as MSM under NACP, were socially and culturally closer to or overlapped with trans* women communities (this in part also reflects how the frameworks for self-identification have changed in the last 25 years in West Bengal among gender and sexual minorities, with queer, genderqueer and gender fluid fast gaining traction and even replacing earlier identity terms). Additionally, gay and bisexual identified men in general have not been inclined to access the services provided by government-supported and CBO-led HIV interventions – possibly out of a sense of deep-seated transphobia, distrust for government services or because of poor outreach efforts on the part of the organizations concerned.

Since 2011, the very existence of traditional interventions has been impacted negatively. In 2011, West Bengal experienced a change of political regime (as mentioned earlier in the report) for the first time in more than three decades. It may be mere coincidence but along with major changes in the power structures in the state administration, a number of HIV interventions were closed down on various grounds in the next few years. These included almost all the interventions serving MSM and trans* women, which till date have not been re-opened or replaced with new interventions. Apart from abruptly leaving community members registered with these interventions without access to information or services, these closures also impacted the incomes and well-being of the large outreach workforces engaged in the interventions. Last year, Project Pehchan too came to an end without much possibility of a revival or, as mentioned earlier, making a substantial and sustainable mark on the functioning of the national and state HIV responses. So far there have been no assessments of how these developments may have affected the sexual health of MSM and trans* women, especially in terms of HIV prevalence and HIV treatment access and adherence.

The last five years have also seen the NACP itself losing ground. Premature elation over recent successes in reduction of parent to child transmission of HIV and an ill-planned integration with the National Rural Health Mission have been cited as reasons. While the concept of horizontal integration (as against vertical health programmes) maybe workable for the larger community, it cannot succeed in the context of highly stigmatized and criminalized communities whose members cannot simply walk in into health facilities and avail of services without experiencing denial or bias – perhaps manifested in being unable to discuss their real and pressing sexual health needs in frank terms. Traditional targeted interventions, despite all their shortcomings, did play a role in bridging the gap between government and private health services and the communities concerned and ensuring delivery and uptake of services. A recent concerted civil society campaign has assured a continuation of the traditional HIV interventions, even if downsized, beyond the current (fourth) and next phases of NACP (Mishra, 2016). This, however, is no assurance about the quality of the interventions, guarantee against stock-outs of condoms or drugs, or timely payments to intervention staff.

On the more positive front, Kolkata continues to host the oldest queer pride walk in India and South Asia (it hosted the first in 1999). Its neighbour Chandannagar and other towns too host the pride walk, making West Bengal one of the few states to have multiple pride walk sites. Kolkata city has also seen a growth in queer cultural and academic spaces since the early 2000s, prominent among which have been film productions and festivals, art exhibitions, and a variety of gender and sexuality themed events in public places.[7] Educational institutions too have been opening up to dialogue on gender and sexuality. Equally, queer visibility in online spaces has increased through webzines like Varta and a host of social media forums in different languages and covering different regions of West Bengal. Some of these forums have offline community activities as

---

[7] Talks and Interfaces column in Varta webzine: http://www.vartagensex.org/talks.php (last accessed December 7, 2016.

well (Swar and Harmless Hugs), while other forums have expanded the dialogue on queer and sexual health issues into newer areas (Kinky Collective and The Consentwalas). These developments have always offered 'alternatives' to traditional HIV interventions in terms of access to sexual health in the broader sense. Today, more so than ever before, they (especially the online forums along with the use of digital technologies like the smart phone) have the potential to majorly change the way better sexual health can be 'achieved' or 'enjoyed' by MSM and trans* women across socio-economic divisions.

Case Study

SAATHII experience with support from Alliance India under Project Pehchan: In 2013-14, SAATHII implemented a pilot project in Bhadrak, Odisha on using mobile phones to convey basic messages on gender, sexuality, sexual health, legal rights, education/skills building and career development to adolescent MSM and trans* women below 18 years of age. The project aimed at reaching out to a population neglected by the traditional HIV interventions (which are limited to adult individuals) and youth programmes (which are rarely inclusive of adolescents with non-normative genders and sexualities). While the National AIDS Control Programme at that stage was silent about covering 'most at risk populations' among the youth, the Odisha State Youth Policy and the Reproductive and Maternal, Newborn, Child and Adolescent Health Policy of 2013 were more inclusive in their mandates, with the former specifically mentioning the need to work with LGBT youth.

While the project had a policy back-up, the challenge was to reach out to the adolescents in an ethical manner without involving their parents/guardians. Going by the ICMR guidelines that parental involvement can be bypassed if it is in the best interest of the child (that is, if parental involvement is likely to act as a barrier to information/service provision on crucial life and health matters), the project mobilized around 125 adolescent MSM and trans* women who owned personal mobile phones through traditional outreach methods and then enrolled them onto the mobile outreach programme.

Parallel to this, 6-8 community peers were involved in consultations to develop relevant messages and these were vetted through another multi-stakeholder consultation that involved NGOs/CBOs working with MSM and trans* women in Bhadrak; NGOs and government agencies (including Child Welfare Committees and Childline among others) working with youth populations (including Odisha State AIDS Control Society); and private sector agencies involved in providing vocational training in Bhadrak. This consultation also helped develop cross-linkages between agencies working with MSM and trans* women and those working with youth populations.

Next, SAATHII utilized a TRAI-approved SMS package available online that allowed a specific number of free messages (in Odia but using English script) to be sent out every day through a designated phone number. The dissemination of messages was carried out over two to three months, and then evaluated. Around 20% of the message recipients availed of the various sexual health and youth service provider referral linkages that had been developed as part of the project. There were some drop-outs from the programme, but the overall feedback from the message recipients was positive and the project seemed to have considerable potential. OSACS wanted SAATHII to replicate the programme among schools in the district, but there were limited resources available and donor support for the pilot did not continue.

CHAPTER 3

DIGITAL MEDIA AND SEXUAL HEALTH

Despite the decline in adult HIV prevalence in India, which has seen HIV prevalence among adults drop from 0.41% in 2001 to 0.26% in 2014-2015 according to the National Integrated Biological and Behavioural surveillance conducted by NACO; new HIV infections among MSM and trans* populations hasn't shown as steady of a decline (NACO 2009, 2014). National surveillance data from the National AIDS Control Organisation provides evidence that the MSM populations have a high HIV prevalence rate of 4.3% (NACO, 2014), which is more than twenty times that of the general population (NACP IV, 2011). West Bengal, along with Jharkhand and Odisha, accounts for a prevalence of 6.70% (NACO, 2014). Globally, it has been reported that despite the scale up of targeted HIV prevention to gay men, other MSM and trans*s, entrenched stigma and discrimination impede prevention efforts, resulting in proportionately higher HIV incidence among these vulnerable groups. Although 5-10% of HIV infection worldwide is attributed to MSM, only 1.2% of the entire funding for HIV prevention is geared towards this group (MSMGF, 2010), making it one of the most underfunded groups among populations at risk.

Violence, stigma and discrimination make it difficult not only to estimate HIV sero prevalence accurately, but also create challenges for effective HIV education and prevention among gay men, other

MSM and trans*s in India (Chakrapani, Newman and Shunmugam, 2008). Internationally, evidence of human rights violations against sexual minorities and HIV and AIDS peer outreach workers in community and healthcare contexts continues to exist (Gutierrez et al., 2010). Research further suggests that despite the continued mobilisation of marginalised communities to challenge stigma and discrimination, changing the wider social context requires building more effective and targeted structural change approaches to reduce HIV infections among MSM and trans* communities (Campbell and Cornish, 2010: MSMGF, 2010). In addition, as Dhall and Boyce (2015) have argued more recently economic exclusion remains a major contributing factor to HIV vulnerability. They argue:

> The issue of economic inclusion for people with non-normative genders and sexualities is therefore complex and embedded with myriad challenges, relating for example to socioeconomic precarity relating to sexual and gender non-conformity, poor health-care conditions and difficult legislative environment. (Dhall and Boyce, 2015: 16)

Gay men and other men who have sex with men and trans* people who do not necessarily identify as 'gay' or 'MSM' remain hidden to HIV prevention and outreach programmes (Boyce, 2007; Deb et al, 2009). Married men who have sex with men also remain 'hidden', often not receiving sexual health and HIV prevention information. As our observation and working with the National AIDS Control Program (NACP) in India have shown, the section of MSM that remains most left out are male sexual partners of *kothis*[8]. These groups frequently remain outside targeted HIV prevention

[8] Narrain (2004: 2-3) explains that '*Kothi* is a feminised male identity which is adopted by some people in the Indian subcontinent and is marked by gender non-conformity. *Kothis* though biologically male, adopts feminine modes of dressing, speech and behaviour and would look for a male partner who has masculine modes of behaviour.' Their male partners are called *panthis*. Interestingly, *kothis* are grouped under MSM by NACO (National Aids Control Organisation), but at the community level they identify more with trans women.

because it is hard to reach them (Ramakrishnan, 2007). Despite the targeted interventions provided for visible gay men, other MSM and trans* communities (NACO, 2014) certain groups, due their invisibility, remain at higher risk for HIV infection.

It is also important to note that we view the continued use of the normative categories of 'MSM' and 'trans*' as problematic when the individuals being referred to can find these terms irrelevant. While we use them in this report, our experience suggests it is hard to believe in a singular 'MSM' or 'trans*' category with a homogenized experience. Thus, we use these terms only because they are the dominant tropes, recognising they are specific subjectivities indexed by the fields of power of HIV and international development research and policy (Gosine, 2009). In this book, we draw on the contextual backdrop presented above to consider how the use of digital media and the internet can reach out to multiple audiences and particular groups of gay men, men who have sex with men and trans* people who remain 'hidden' or invisible.

A key challenge to the impact of existing HIV prevention approaches has been the widespread impact of the internet on gay men, other MSM and trans* communities. This is especially true in India with its ubiquitous access to the internet at home and in public internet cafes. Many MSM in Kolkata and across India access the internet as a major resource in helping them acknowledge and 'gather more information about their sexuality' (Sahani, 2008). Popular websites such as PlanetRomeo and Grindr work to shape sexual expectations, norms and practices of gay men, other MSM and trans* (Silveira, 2010). These popular sites are used for socialising and 'hooking up' and provide anonymity for users who do not want to disclose their sexuality.

Shaw (1997) points out that whilst heterosexual people have access to participate in conversations outside the chatroom, for example the bar or a store to find a potential sex partner, not as many opportunities and options exist for homosexual or *queer* people. The chatroom, and by extension the internet, provides the means for queer people to meet and socialise instantaneously. Following Shaw's line of enquiry Mowlabocus (2010) points out that this relationship between the online world created by new media technologies and the offline world of an existing gay male sub culture complicates the questions concerning the character of online communities and identities. He says that 'the digital is not separate from other spheres of gay life, but in fact grows out of while remaining rooted in, local, national and international gay male subculture' (p. 7).

Mowlabocus's statement about the digital being rooted in local gay male subcultures is important in understanding queer cyberspace. Whilst anti-discrimination laws exist on a national level in the United Kingdom, in some countries in Europe, and parts of the United States of America, sodomy laws still exist in many parts of the world especially in South Asia as a remnant of the colonisers.[9] Prior research in India has shown how digital spaces have evolved and changed perceptions of cruising, anonymity and safe sex (Dasgupta, 2014; Dasgupta, 2015; Dasgupta, 2016; Singh, 2016). In recent years, internet social networking and dating sites have begun to take sexual health information and awareness seriously (Mowlabocus, 2010; Clift, 2010). As Figure 1 below shows, PlanetRomeo regularly hosts discussions on sexual health issues including HIV prevention. Both PlanetRomeo and Gaydar have started making sexual health information prominently available on their website (Also see Focus Group 1 Discussion in appendices). Planet Romeo announced in 2009 that they would only offer porn films for download which depict safer sex and have explicitly stated they will not endorse or host bareback porn films for their users.

---

[9] Homosexuality is currently illegal in Afghanistan, Bangladesh, Bhutan, Pakistan and Sri Lanka in South Asia, with only Nepal legalising homosexuality in 2007. India legalised homosexuality in 2009 following a judgement by the Delhi High Court, only to recriminalize it in 2013 by the Supreme Court. In addition, seven countries (which include, Iran, Saudi Arabia, UAE, Nigeria, Mauritania, Sudan and Yemen) punish homosexuality with the death penalty.

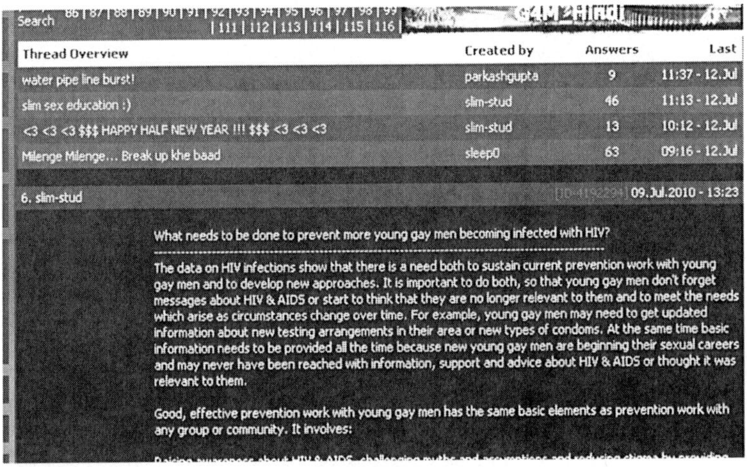

Figure 1: Planet Romeo India Discussion Forum

Little critical analysis exists in the research literature to develop the evidence on the use and impact of these informal digital HIV prevention approaches or the extent to which they prevent/do not prevent new infections. To date, there has not been a serious effort to link these types of intervention with large scale public health and face-to-face community mobilisation efforts in India. Furthermore, these commercial websites (such as Planet Romeo and Grindr) lack a sustainable commitment to fighting stigma and discrimination and do not make available critical online educational opportunities. This suggests a need for context-specific community-based and led HIV prevention and education approaches (within the context specifically of India) using digital media and the internet to develop theoretically-informed structural change approaches for community strengthening towards HIV prevention (Singh and Walsh, 2012).

Another significant aspect of queer lives in India is their stratified existence based on class dynamics (Dasgupta, 2014; Gupta, 2015). Gupta (2005) explains the frustration faced by many *kothis* in mainstream society, where money and the ability to speak English dictate social boundaries. This makes it difficult for gay, MSM and trans* men who cannot speak English to interact with others in many online spaces. From our observations of and participation in Facebook conversations, it's true that some Facebook spaces are exclusionary on linguistic lines, however there are also other groups which target specific non metropolitan vernacular/non English speaking populace. Facebook and WhatsApp are becoming better with regard to Indian scripts. So there are increasing online interactions in Bengali or Hindi in Kolkata as well as other districts of West Bengal. So in that sense online spaces no longer need be bound by the diktats of English.

This is where we believe digital media and the internet can meet the challenges of HIV prevention for these communities. We believe there is a critical need to address the intersection of HIV prevention with the lived experiences of violence, stigma and discrimination against visible and invisible gay men, other MSM and trans* communities. This is particularly paramount in light of increasing internet ubiquity across the country.

Virtual spaces have the potential for greater deterritorialisation and the performance of productive identities (Wakeford, 1997; Campbell, 2004; Mowlabocus, 2008, 2010). Wakeford (1997) citing Kira Hall and Judith Butler sees identity as fluid and performative and the cyberspace as a place 'where you can be whoever you want to be' (Ibid., p. 25) and also iterating the same physical world differences and prejudices. Butler (1999), writing about this performativity says, 'practices in both homosexual and heterosexual contexts...open surfaces and orifices to erotic signification or close down others [and] effectively reinscribe the boundaries of the body along new cultural lines' (1999, p. 169).

In addition, Mclelland (2002) and Mowlabocus (2010) argue that virtual spaces can break down social and cultural boundaries. As such, virtual spaces can provide a safe space for performance of identities to make new practical knowledge and sensitivity about HIV risk. These approaches have been tried with MSM and trans* women in Thailand (Walsh, 2008; Walsh, Lasky and Morrish, 2011; Chaiyajit and Walsh, 2012). This prior research has potential for use in India, as it implies that digital HIV prevention and education can affect and respect agency, while situated in the sexual and social practices of gay men, other MSM and trans* women, in ways that traditional approaches such as workshops may not.

There is a small but growing body of literature that reports on similar attempts to respond to recent shifts in gay male sexual cultures. While some (Welfare &Lighton, 2011) urge caution in pursuing online forms of community outreach, others have identified significant benefits in utilising digital platforms for work with MSM communities (also see McGlotten, 2007, 2013; Mowlabocus, 2010, Mowlabocus et al, 2014,2015,2016; Mitra, 2010. Rosser et al. (2011) have proven that digitally-mediated methods of outreach increase the speed, depth and honesty of service user disclosure, compared to offline forms of engagement. This is particularly true in relation to the disclosure of sensitive or stigmatised issues such as unprotected sexual contact, risk-taking behaviours (including drug use during sex) and partner concordance.

Meanwhile, Landers et al. (2011) contend that building solidarity networks with the gay men's health movement on a global scale is key to addressing the challenges that currently face sexual health promotion workers. They contend that most of the health outreach in the US has been focused on HIV/AIDS, however it needs to be recognised that using the discourse of HIV/AIDS to target health advocacy is not always successful as gay MSM and trans* women's health goes beyond the HIV/AIDS narrative, further arguing that such policies are often enmeshed within funding and government strategies which often limit the levels within which outreach can take place. They argue that such solidarity networking requires deeper engagement with digital forms of communication, which moves activists and workers outside of the local silos in which they work and connect them up to a broader population peer mentors. Supporting this claim, Pedrana et al. (2013) found that an intervention model built around online videos hosted on the social media platform Youtube, was accessed by men from across the world, including both the UK and Saudia Arabia. Pedrana et al evaluated the QAF (Queer as F***) project, which delivers sexual health promotion through short webisodes on SNS (social networking sites) to gay men. The webisodes are uploaded on Facebook and Youtube. The primary aims of QAF wereto reach out to gay and bisexual men to improve their knowledge on sexual health issues and evaluating health promotion interventions on SNS. This study used a mixed method process through which data collection was done through various ways. Statistics were collected from Youtube and Facebook to monitor usage data, interactivity of the users was collected through scrapbook entries, finally focus groups were conducted for more in-depth information on engagement with the series. Interviews with MSM who engaged with the intervention revealed that the location of the videos (on a social media platform) provided men with an added impetus to discuss sexual health issues. One solution that Landers et al outline is building solidarity networks with the gay men's health movement on a global scale and coordinating agency wide efforts in consultation with the gay community themselves an especially the gay youth who need to be mobilised:

> And there must be special emphasis placed on the importance of nurturing young leaders to take this movement beyond the current field of vision. Tapping into the creativity and boundless energy of young gay, bisexual and transgender men in our community will ensure the movement thrives and remains relevant. (Landers et al, 2011: S106).

This model of nurturing young leaders within the community has been undertaken in another interesting study within the Afro-American gay community in the US, where SNS (social networking sites) such as Facebook were deployed to train and create sexual health advocates for the community. Digitally enabled networks and sites of communication and sharing are vital to the development of youth advocates and community sexual health 'champions' according to Young and Jaganathan (2014). Their claims are based on a feasibility study involving 55 MSM recruited to a 'secret' Facebook group in which eight peer leaders sought to facilitate and support user engagement. Of particular note is their finding that the Latino population (accounting for 60% of the cohort) accounted for 82% of the activity in the forum whereas the African-American population (making up almost 40% of the cohort) accounted for only 25.5% of the user engagement. These findings serve to underscore the need to consider each target demographic on their own terms, and demands that health promotion agencies recognise that a 'one-size-fits-all' model of community outreach simply does not work. Of particular relevance here, is the finding that only 21% of the Facebook conversations that took place during the research period focused directly on sexual health. Personal conversations about user identity and sexual orientation featured more regularly. Interestingly this study found that age was not very important in influencing the group participation (6), which is a common issue raised about such interventions. The paper also mentions that whilst age and baseline health had nothing to do with participation, it was found that racial differences did, something that outreach workers need to be aware of both online as well as offline. Furthermore, participants only initiated 37% of conversations that took place in the group, identifying the need for peer outreach workers to be online and engaged regularly, initiating and sustaining 'relevant' conversations with the group members.

A similar conversation based approach was also undertaken by Rhodes et al. (2007) who have reported on a chat-room based intervention programme on two digital sites populated by MSM. Their results identify the potential success of such programmes, while also identifying the fact that those who are at the highest risk of HIV exposure failed to engage with the intervention. In short, some, but by no means all, MSM engaged with this online intervention. Meanwhile, Macmaster et al. (2003) report on a six-month pilot projectbased in San Jose, California, and which provided an outreach service to MSM via chat rooms dedicated to MSM. The study identified the key role that timing plays in such intervention work, with the highest success rate for user engagement being during lunch hours and between 12:00 and 17:00 on weekends. The study identified the challenges that the outreach team faced when trying to engage users during the evening when it was assumed the target population were more interested in using the chatrooms for their primary purpose – to arrange real-time physical hook ups.

Collectively, the results of these studies demonstrate the feasibility and potential utility of using social networking technologies for health education and promotion. At the same time, these studies report on community outreach programmes that develop specific platforms, spaces or services in which to place the intervention. As such, they all operate 'outside' of MSM-dedicated spaces. This is a departure from the ethos of conventional community outreach and as such, the opportunities for sustainability and further recruitment remain somewhat limited.

CHAPTER 4

RESEARCH SCHEMA

In this section we provide an overview of the research schema and methods that were employed by this research project. A qualitative approach has been utilised, which seeks to allow for the self-expression of informants and interlocutors along with drawing on experience and observations over time – including both in on-line and off-line social worlds. Bryman (2008: 366) argues that 'Qualitative research is a research strategy that usually emphasizes words rather than quantification in the collection and analysis of data.' Further Sandelowski (2004) writing about the advantages of qualitative research notes that it is a way of discovering how human beings understand, experience, interpret, and produce the social world. As noted above, words might express different realities, dependent on context, intionality and so on.

The researchers have observed and taken part in sexual health intervention programs over a long period of time and in various capacities. Boyce and Dhall have been involved with ground level intervention programs for over twenty years (See Dhall, 2005; Boyce, 2007). They have both facilitated and observed outreach work in Kolkata and other urban and suburban areas of Eastern India. Such work has blurred the lines between intervention and research, much in the way that ethnographic method might be seen to open contextual spaces in research projects that prevail against the formal parameters of some other research methods. Boyce in particular is an ethnographer – having worked in West Bengal periodically over a number of years in this way. Dhall has been working as a community organiser and sexual health activist for over two decades and was able to mobilise support from several organisations and individuals for this project. Dasgupta undertook digital ethnography through 'lurking' (Mowlabocus, 2010) on PlanetRomeo and Grindr and also engaging with users on these sites to ask them about safe sex practices.

Digital ethnography in this case encapsulates what is happening on social networking sites and mobile applications and immerse oneself within that digital culture. It is about studying the digital technology as much as it is about studying the ways people use it. As Markham (2016) argues: 'Everyday lived experience in this decade is impacted by the convergence of media, the mediation and remediation of identities, and the still-rising interest in quantification and big data'. Dasgupta spent around 40 hours over two weeks on PlanetRomeo and Grindr, two of the most popular queer male social and dating application/sites in Kolkata, observing profiles, conversations and any developer advertised sexual health messages that were being broadcast.

Focus Groups and Interviews were an important component of the present research project. A total of four focus groups took place with around 10 participants. All three researchers in collaboration developed the focus group transcript and questions. Each participant was offered two hundred rupees (approximately £3) for travel expenses. Each focus group lasted between one and two hours. These focus groups were transcribed and analysed by all three members of the research team. In addition the researchers also conducted informal unstructured interviews which were written down as research notes.

Symposium and Workshop

A one day workshop and symposium was conducted at Jadavpur University, Kolkata on 24th August, 2016 where the research team presented sections from this research to an audience of 50 made up of sexual health activists and academics. In addition a total of 15 papers were also invited on themes of sexuality, media narratives and health to facilitate a wider discussion on some of the issues that the research team uncovered during the project. Detailed notes were also taken of the discussions on this day and kept by the research team which was then used during the analysis phase of the project.

The research team produced detailed notes about their observations and the focus groups were transcribed (see the detailed edited transcripts in the appendix of this book). After this, a process of coding took place. Coding is the process of examining the raw qualitative data which were in the form of words, images, phrases, sentences or paragraphs to which codes or labels (based on themes and emerging research questions) were assigned. The codes developed were in terms of main categories and subsidiary ones. In terms of the main categories some of the emerging themes were in the areas of digital literacy, expertise, social stigma and class. Subsidiary categories emerged such as demography, ageism, and language barriers. A process of descriptive coding took place. Before moving on to presenting some of the findings from this research it is imperative to mention that this research was grounded within a strong ethical framework. Other than applying to the University of Southampton for ethical clearance, the researchers also took additional measures to mitigate any issues that might arise during the research process.

Ethics

1. *Anonymity:* For the digital ethnography, only data that was accessible to the researcher was used and all identifying information were deleted or encoded immediately after the data was downloaded. The same was done for the focus groups and interviews. After the participants signed the consent forms, their recordings were assigned a pseudonym. All researchers agreed that when accessing the data sets they would not attempt to re-identify subjects or

disclose any identities that might be inadvertently re-identified, or otherwise to compromise the privacy of the subjects.

2. Need for Support, Information or Indication of Harm: During the course of the focus groups, we anticipated that participants may highlight a potential need, or we may feel that they would benefit from additional support or information. In both case we compiled a referrals list for issues that might arise during the course of an interview. These included emergency, sexual health, mental health and emotional support, and counselling.
3. Power in the Research Relationship: The focus groups were designed to be open-ended, flexible and conversational in nature in order to allow the participants to tell their story in their own 'voice', and as they would want. However, due to the in-depth and spontaneous nature of focus group discussions there was always the potential for participants to reveal personal, private, and sensitive information, which they perhaps did not anticipate. Participants were given the option for withdrawing any sections that they did not want included. Every attempt was made to create a comfortable non-judgmental atmosphere, and the researchers remained responsive and empathic listeners. We also used language that was suitable. Depending on our participants we chose to speak in English or a mixture of English, Bengali and Hindi.
4. Representation: We were also aware that some participants might be concerned with how they would be represented to wider audiences in the writing up of the research and its dissemination. We reminded them that their identity would be protected in publications or other methods of dissemination by referring to them with a pseudonym of their choosing, and changing or removing any other identifying information (where they live, work, socialise, names of family members or friends). Every effort has been made to represent participants accurately. All participants were also reminded that they would be given a copy of the overall research findings.

In the next section we outline some of the key findings from this research project, which is based on the ethnography, participant observations, focus groups, interviews and the workshop/symposium.

CHAPTER 5

KEY FINDINGS

Sexual Health Promotion

Sexual health promotion can be defined as the various ways through which one can achieve a reduction in sexual health inequalities. As our research has shown, these affect all ages and all parts of the society with a higher concentration of inequalities towards MSM, gay and trans* individuals (see chapter 2 and 3). There are is some specific differences here in terms on class and region (see Dasgupta, 2014 and Focus Group Discussion 2). Whilst there have been several programs that have been designed around MSM, gay and trans* people, the ways in which sexual health promotion is understood by them varies. As one respondent pointed out:

> BPB: What I feel sexual health is that it is about safe sexual practices. The absence of these practices leads to a variety of complications and problem, often leading to something major. If a person is well informed about safe sexual practices and can make them a part of his daily life, then he is likely to have good sexual health.

Another respondent was in agreement with this definition and added:

> DGM: I agree… Sexual health means sexual awareness and safe sexual behaviours.

Other respondents agreed that despite much investment towards sexual health projects and intervention from the government initiatives to the NGO led programs there remained a significant gap.

Sexual health and sex education in India remains a contested terrain and in fact in 2014, a health minister went so far as to suggest banning sex education from the curriculum altogether.[10] Several States have also been at the forefront opposing this on grounds of it being 'impure', 'outrageous' and 'unfit for Indian society' with some leaders even suggesting an abstinence only program instead.[11] Despite several of these roadblocks our research suggest that sexual health promotion when started as at an early age engenders critical discussion on issues such as homosexuality and sexual health and also informs choices in later life. One such campaign which a lot of our respondents mentioned in the context of West Bengal was the Bula-di campaign which was run by the West Bengal State AIDS Prevention and Control Society.

Figure 2: Bula Di Campaign

The campaign capitalised on the familiarity of the *didi* (older sister) figure in Bengali society, who in a non-threatening way

---

[10] See https://www.youtube.com/watch?v=EiIxkOah09E

[11] See: http://news.bbc.co.uk/1/hi/world/south_asia/6949714.stm

educated the West Bengal public about HIV/AIDS and provided a confidential helpline for people to get in touch. The campaign made good use of media convergence (Jenkins, 2009) using billboards, television advertisements, radio commercials and posters, and mobile media (through a toll free number offering advice). In fact this was the single most popular campaign which used a customised approach to target specifically the Bengali community. One of our respondents RB says:

> RB: When I was in school life, this Bula-di thing was going on. I was maybe 7 or 8, and at that time I did not have an idea actually what is a condom, and they used to distribute condoms around my school and in the neighbourhood around my school, so I just got caught up and like there were people who just took it for fun to see what it is, and that was the first time that I saw a condom. So after that I started – I asked my parents why they are doing this, why they are distributing, so that was the first idea, I had any idea like people talking about sexual health – that was – I think that was effective at some point, but I think that really did not have much outreach, though the Bula-di campaign was really accepted throughout the country, but because of its like very – it was not much layered and it had lot to say but it was not at all vulgar, which was much fit for the Indian audience, so I think that I liked that.

However as RB further argued, the Bula-di campaign emphasised a lot on condom usage, primarily targeting heterosexual men. It did not necessarily have a specific message for MSM, gay men or trans* people, but did locate the role of condoms in sexual health. Several respondents felt that 'information was key' to successful peer outreach. Other respondents such as SG have elaborated that successful sexual health intervention strategies need to also include governmental initiatives.

> SJ: In the context of sexual health for the MTH [MSM,

> transgender, hijra]population is like getting services from the government hospitals - on sexual and reproductive health, like getting access on the condoms, lubricants and talk about their sexual activities and behaviour with the doctors, who should have the knowledge of the MTH issues, and their sexual health and rights. So, this is my perception of the sexual health.

Several respondents also mentioned sexual health being directly linked to mental health and wellbeing. Social stigma and continued anxiety over the ability to access sexual health materials remains a major cause for several gay, MSM and trans* men from seeking care and advice. The 2013 judgement which we mentioned earlier that has recriminalized same sex non reproductive sexual intercourse has once again put queer rights at the very back of 'liberal' India's priorities. This has also seen a reduction in the number of people who are being approached for sexual health advocacy. One respondent (RL) for example clarified that he was too scared to bring back sexual health material home as he was not 'out' to his parents, thus he was dependant solely on trying to find relevant information online, making it critical for peer outreach workers to be developing new forms of outreach and advocacy programs targeted at people who are increasingly accessing them online. Whilst not directly related to the IPC 377 judgement the changing mind sets that the Supreme Court decision could have brought about has been dashed once again. AH agrees that new forms of counselling using social media need to be developed:

> AH: ...So that is a bit of a counselling over email or through a chat. Some of them say that from this day, from this hour to this hour, our counsellor would be sitting online for a web chat. So people can post questions and we can have this kind of a group discussion session. Some places I've heard that people can also do one-to-one web chat or even Skype chat. So that is also a possibility.

A final aspect of sexual health promotion which has received little critical attention is the role of it as immaterial labour. Immaterial labour is an academic term used to describe the affective and cognitive commodities produced by work that exist outside the traditional wage-based consideration of labour as a material-commodity-producing activity, as well as the activity of producing this new form of commodity (see McRobbie, 2010; Terranova, 2004). Whilst several respondents we spoke to are paid outreach workers, a good number of them are volunteers and do this on their own time, 'wanting to make a difference'. Whilst Marx recognised the value of aesthetic meanings through the labour of creative people, this was considered marginal and economically insignificant. It is only in recent years through queer and feminist scholarship (McRobbie, 2010) when the value and productivity of housework has gained significant traction. AVD in one of the focus groups mentioned about the importance of profile creation and website creation for it to be able to gain the trust of potential users.

Digital Literacy

One of the key issues which this study brought up was the issue of digital literacy. Digital literacy as we understand it is the knowledge, skills and practices that are required to use a broad range of digital devices such as computers, laptops and mobile phones. Digital literacy in India remains a key area for development. The current Prime Minister Narendra Modi said: 'Digital India is our dream for the nation. When I say "digital India" it is not for the rich but for those who are poor'. Keeping this ethos in mind, the National Digital Literacy Mission was set up through the Ministry of Electronics and Information Technology which currently has 1,958 training partners and an estimated 99,56,632 individuals enrolled for training.[12] The ministry defines digital literacy as the ability of individuals and communities to understand and use digital technologies for meaningful actions within life situations. The

[12] Information about this is available here: http://ndlm.in/overview-of-ndlm.html (Accessed on 01 November, 2016)

training which is made available to anyone between the ages of 14 and 60 is free to those coming from Scheduled Caste and Scheduled Tribe backgrounds and a nominal cost of 125 INR (£2) for all others with instruction made available in local languages.

In the context of this present project, we unpack digital literacy to not just mean understanding how certain digital mediums work, but also issues around language (English being the most predominant language through which these digital medium operate) and that of media affordance. We view technologies as artefacts that may both be shaped by and shape the practices of human beings who interact with and through them. Hutchby (2001: 444) defines affordances as 'functional and relational aspects which frame, while not determining, the possibilities for agentic action in relation to an object'. Consider this statement from SS:

> SS: . . . Everything has two sides to it – I found it very funny that our boys and girls who find it so difficult to write in Bangla were writing English thanks to Facebook – basically Bangla words written in English script. Some of them now talk so fluently in meetings, they've started using English words and typing in English. So these are the positive aspects of Facebook. Similarly, a website can have such positive options. Now technology has moved on, so maybe we should also deploy it for our benefit.

Digital literacy in this context is thus also being able to navigate various sites and understanding the technological affordance of how best to use that site to relay a message or information. At the same time the kinds of mediums that are used to get the message across need to also be customised for the different groups and communities that are being targeted. For example AH says:

> AH: Actually you need to publicize it through multiple modes because – I'll again go to the example of a 17 year old boy, who doesn't know PlanetRomeo or Grindr, what he'll do is do a Google search for gay issues or something like that. So if

you put this [helpline]number within, let's say PlanetRomeo or Grindr, this guy is never going to find this number. On the other hand, for a hijra population, who would not do a Google search, she would only come to know this number if it is on a leaflet distributed in a public event by an NGO or a CBO or during a rally or maybe some other event.

Another respondent also mentioned that mainstream media could be used in those areas where the penetration of digital media was still low, which was agreed by the other participants.

SG: Or maybe television advertisements. . .

AH: . . . or television ads. For some populations, for example, working class males in suburban areas who do not have so much of access to internet, maybe small posters on trains or publicity on platforms would be the only source of reaching to them.

And yet the penetration of technology is growing and can't be under-estimated:

AD: And as SR said, in places like Malda, this issue [of few people using smart phones] will be applicable. But, even on the escort site I mentioned earlier, there are people from remote interiors. Someone from Bamungachi or Habra had contacted me – and he wasn't smart looking in the way we usually understand – but he found me and contacted me through the escort site. So sometimes we have pre-conceived ideas . . .

Participants also mentioned that applications such as WhatsApp where small groups of users can be created and Youtube are also good platforms to use for reaching out to wider people. Whatsapp currently has close to 50 million users in India and as several of our respondents claimed has overtaken text messages owing to cheaper data packages and unlimited word length for the messages. Youtube was also mentioned as another preferred platform. Burgess and Green (2009) have called Youtube a dynamic cultural system whose technological affordance enables active cultural participation.

> SG: And WhatsApp, AH was saying, WhatsApp groups even became very popular in WhatsApp separately, and I was talking about Youtube, because small documentaries – small series, LGBT specific any information or maybe any pride walk related documentary – even students and youth are making those films and small documents and uploading on Youtube and among friends it becomes very popular . . .

Youtube as a participatory platform provides a space for individuals and community groups to make low cost films and distribute it for a global audience. This kind of user created content and accessibility shifts the power relations between media industries and their consumers allowing new forms of debates and information to emerge and circulate. Alexander and Losh (2010) have also written about the role Youtube has played in recent years helping young queer people to 'come out' within a supportive space (also see Drushel, 2010; Driver, 2005). Social media and hooking up services such as Grindr are making use of youtube through hyperlinks to 'educate' users about HIV and sexual health in India (for example see Figure 3).

This is an area that will benefit from greater community mobilisation and NGO support. These are platforms which require relatively little digital literacy skills and groups such as Varta Trust are in the process of training outreach workers, sexuality and health activists to use these platforms usefully for their campaigns. As one respondent explained, there are several spaces which are not being targeted for sexual health intervention and social media is one of them:

> AH: These are all the places that current interventions are not addressing, for example, private spaces where private parties are happening, sexual or massage set-ups in massage parlours,

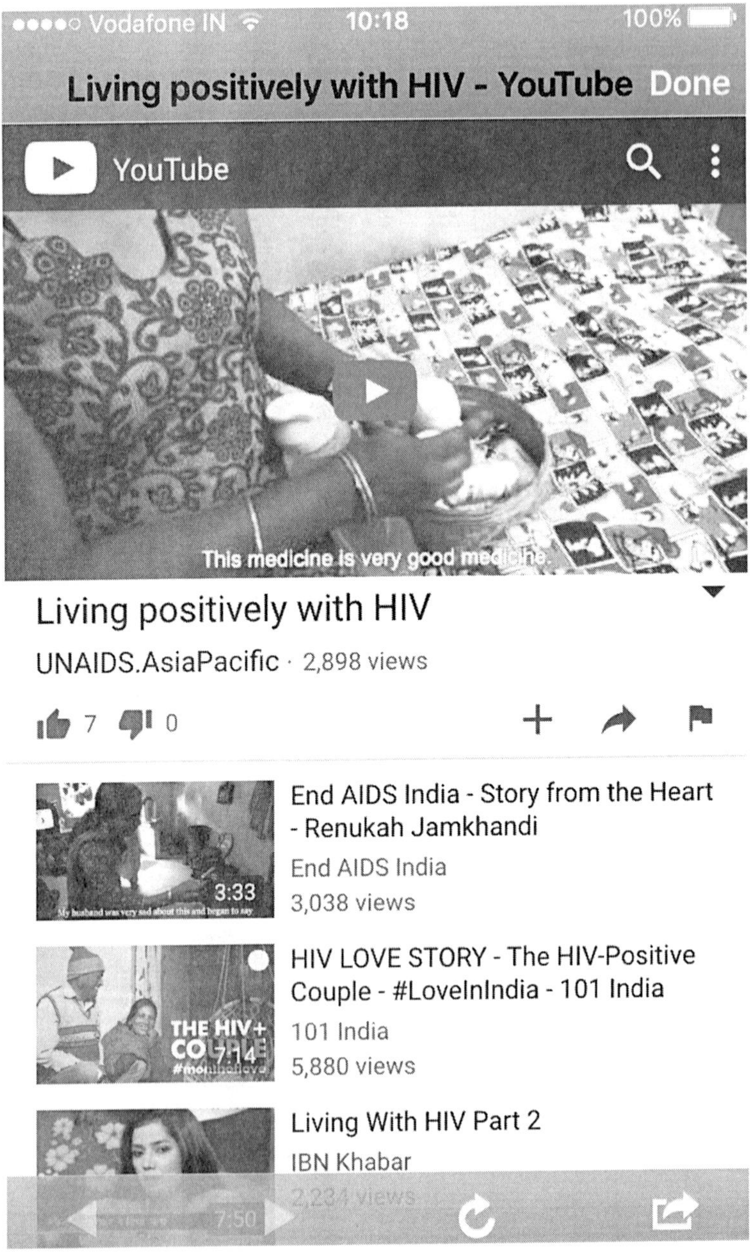

Figure 3: Youtube Videos Embedded and Hyperlinked through Grindr

> the entire space about online dating apps, there are no health interventions going on. In some of the dating forums or dating sites, there are advice columns, or people write a post, but that has a very limited effect or impact.

Digital literacy is also related to providing 'customised' services for different platforms. For example, some respondents argued how trying to provide information on sites such as PlanetRomeo often got them blocked. They came across as too 'medical', whereas if this information was being provided somewhere like Facebook, users would be much more receptive to that.

Expertise and Trust

Trust is a key issue for many of our respondents. The passage of the Supreme Court decision (see Dasgupta, 2015) on Section 377 recriminalising non procreative/peno vaginal sex and its social ramifications on the queer community have been great. It has led to an increase in social and cultural stigma and the fear of legal ramifications if people were to describe how they might have had unsafe sex. Several respondents have argued that many doctors are homophobic and there is a sense of discomfort trying to solicit sexual health advice from them. As RB explains:

> RB: I think there is a gap, and when you go to this ICTC thing like for check-up and all that, the way they behave is terrible, and if you do not belong to the mainstream, and if you belong to someone from alternative sexuality, they will behave like as if you are something else and untouchable, and you have HIV already. So it's very frightening and they would ask unnecessary questions like they would try to emphasize – if it's a kothi or dhurani identity and if they get it, and they would try to know that whether you have slept with a man and that is the main thing that becomes more important for them. Whether you have had sexual intercourse or not that they ask later, you slept with a man, and they behave as if that

> is the only way you can get it, and they don't even talk about blood transfusion and other risks . . .

He further explained that his friends have been threatened with denial to treatment if it was found out that they had sex with a same sex partner.

> RB: And they even say that you can – like I have a friend who said that right after 377 was put off, that thing was again criminalized, this lady on the opposite side said that they can deny treatment if you have slept with a man.

Digital and social media have a significant role to play here as it offers gay, MSM and trans* people a chance to get some preliminary advice or to look up possible sympathetic medical professionals they can get in touch with. With a significant number of queer/qay dating/social sites, it is a long task making sure there is presence in all these spaces. Whilst NGO's and community organisations are yet to make a strong mark in this area, several individual groups have sprung up to take on this challenge. As AVD explained:

> AVD: It was in 2009. . . so we started having a profile on every group which was talking about people who were looking for sexual partners. . . . Individuals, we were not part of NGOs but we were a bunch of individuals who thought that this could be done. And so we all had our work because that time I was doing my Masters. Anyway, so whoever had time, we had profiles on those groups. We used to have multiple profiles – I had 40 profiles for 40 different groups and I had to maintain all those profiles, and my job was to monitor whoever is seeking sexual partners, and then I would be going ahead and liking it first and then commenting there 'I'm sure that you're using condoms'.

AVD and his group's activity to sensitise and inform people about safe sex paid off as following the High Court decision of 2009, there was a proliferation of LGBTQ websites and webpages all giving out advice on sexual health. AVD also explained that following the online intervention they were also able to then get some of the users especially vulnerable groups such as sex workers to come and get tested in community organised health camps.

> AVD: We found it's the absolutely best platform to reach out to people. So as I said we started having profiles, then after two years we first conducted our – the first HIV, free HIV test only for gay men and transgender sex workers.

This was based on mutual trust which was developed over time on the social media sites which then transformed into attendance to physical sexual health intervention programs. One of the other central questions of this research was how do service users determine whether the information they are receiving from a website is reliable or not. One respondent argued that if the website giving out the advice belonged to a trusted charity or organisation, they would more likely believe it.

> RB: You see there are – like there is Amitie' Trust, like every NGO who talks about sexuality, alternate sexuality, and even women oriented organizations, they are talking about sexual health and alternate sexualities, and they refer them to various places. The thing is it's not just about knowing HIV issues, condoms and the risks, but it is more important to know that this is just not a disease . . . .

In a further quote, RB elaborates:

> RB: See, first if I go through something like 'Varta', there are many stories I have gone through, I really like them because I found them very relatable. So I thought that somewhere I could see some parts of me in them, and I could make other people of the community read them. I mean there were real life stories, true stories and they were coming from the persons who have faced those issues, and faced those problems – or not just problems, because they are incidents coming

> from their own mouths, so that makes it more authentic, the style, the style of the blog, I took 'Varta' as an example. So it depends on how lucrative and attractive it is, and what style it is written in, how authentic it is, like the sources, the links given; there are certain websites that just have stories and they don't mention any links or back-ups or references from where they have got it. So this is more important I think.

Other respondents felt that it was useful to maybe verify the information that was received on these websites with a visit to the doctor. But having the knowledge beforehand was useful.

> AH: Now my response to that is that at this age and with this much of experience, you're able to question the veracity of the information provided by the site. Now imagine a 16 year old girl or a 17 year old boy, for them that is the information, maybe that person would verify that from his or her friend, but would be hesitant to go to a doctor. But now with your experience you know that I should go to a doctor to verify the information from that source.

One of the other observations our research made and as we explained earlier is to make sure that appropriate messages were being sent on appropriate platforms. For example if there is too many unsolicited sexual health messages being sent on a platform which is primarily for hooking up it would lead to blocking. A more passive response through setting up a dedicated separate page where users could decide to ask for information was much more welcomed.

> AH: Now within these forums also, in Planet Romeo or Grindr, if someone keeps talking about HIV, and very clinically, and keeps on writing then people would, of course, as SG said, they'll be blocking this person. So these messages may have to come sporadically or in a manner which doesn't intrude. So, for example, in Planet Romeo what I've seen is that there HIV messages do not pop up constantly. Sometime

> or the other they'll have a scroll coming up or a pop up coming up but not all the time and every time. Plus there is a dedicated button you can click on that and you can find out more information. So that's not intrusive, so people who do not want that they would not go there.

In terms of trust and privacy, respondents still preferred 'old' technologies such as telephones/mobiles and confidential helplines. As the previous respondent expanded, this was particularly helpful for younger men who would not be able to walk into a government or private hospital to seek advice. Their first port of call for advice would be a helpline. It also provided a more 'human' touch than an electronic mail.

> AH: A phone line provided that anonymity of not revealing your true name, identity, location and that person would not be able to see your face, so with that anonymity there is a lot more confidence in sharing your problems. So actually in SAATHII we saw that the helpline started attracting a lot of people who had a number of medical conditions, and our counsellor had a lot of effort - had to be put in into convincing those people that yes, you need to go and visit a doctor and meet him face-to-face. So for the MTH community, that first point of contact is very necessary where somebody is able to guide, instill a trust in that person that you can go to this doctor, this doctor is gay friendly or TG friendly, this person would not judge you, would not discriminate against you and would protect your confidentiality completely. So that helpline or that email, or that dating app or whatever app has to give that trust. Then only for this community, they would be able to access health services. Or else I'm very sure that a 17, 18, 19 year old guy who realizes that he may have got some infection because of some sex with his partner, would not want to walk into Apollo or to a government hospital and ask for services.

These are also particularly useful for vulnerable communities such as Hijras. As another respondent put it, often people do not say anything in person because of shyness or feeling uncomfortable but they are much more likely to do this over a helpline.

> SG: You have asked about – the question was about what we think about this role of online, digital media in MSM, TG, hijra community – if I talk about hijra community I really have a doubt though how many – about the accessibility of any sites or any social networking sites in regular basis by them, for that reason I must say phone calls zindabad. Still now the helpline is – because unofficially, even me, AH, many people after Pehchan, one of our biggest projects under Global Fund on these community issues, so after Pehchan, even during Pehchan we kept getting calls from them, maybe he's not a client of any of the community groups, he's an individual person, doesn't know about where to get done ICTC, where to go for counselling, where to go for private HIV testing, they do not know. Even if they know, the next question would be like what is the timing, are they community friendly, these are the questions they are not getting answers from anyone, and they feel comfortable talking over phone. So, I have seen the person sitting beside me, talking with me, he didn't utter a single sentence about this issue, but before two days he called me and asked about the ICTC centres. So phone calls, I think are the concrete thing, concrete, proper helpline number circulated to everyone for any sort of support.

Users are also sceptical that if this sort of intervention work gets government funding then there would be massive implication on data safety and confidentiality. They are worried that in the backdrop of Section 377 and the criminalisation of same-sex sex, phone numbers or online profile data that might get captured would lead to legal and social ramification for the service users.

> AH: See (general commotion and laughter) – it's not challenging but there are issues of ethics and confidentiality - that is what is my only concern. For example, tomorrow let's say West Bengal SACS gives this grant to ABC CBO to do this work. So that CBO may set up an interactive voice response system, where all the clients calling their phone numbers get captured. So that is the one obvious thing that you have so many phone numbers coming in. Now imagine if that is not the case and they only take up phone connection from Airtel, Vodafone, whatever and people keep calling. So they may say that we will record the number because we are getting it on our mobile phones. So all these are violating ethics, but these are problematic. Now with email, if people are sending emails, they can take printouts of those emails and file them and say that see so many individual emails came. Now, the government if it really wants to play detective they can go and check the IP address of those emails. So they'll find out so many different IP addresses, but again the ethics and the morality, confidentiality questions come up. Now, if you're talking about dating apps and gay sites, there are so many profiles, the profiles have photographs – of course, there are fake profiles also, but that's the maximum you can validate. But my concern would be for this entire thing all of this violates the main core trust area of confidentiality. So that is the problem.

This has however not stopped social media services such as Grindr in Kolkata to use their platform to let people know about safe sex practices and informing users about sexual health and even providing range of case studies connected to youtube and other platforms where users can get more information and help. This is a significant way in which push messages are also being used in Europe and North America for advertising and letting people know about local services. In addition to providing information, sites such as Grindr can take a more active role participating with local NGO's to

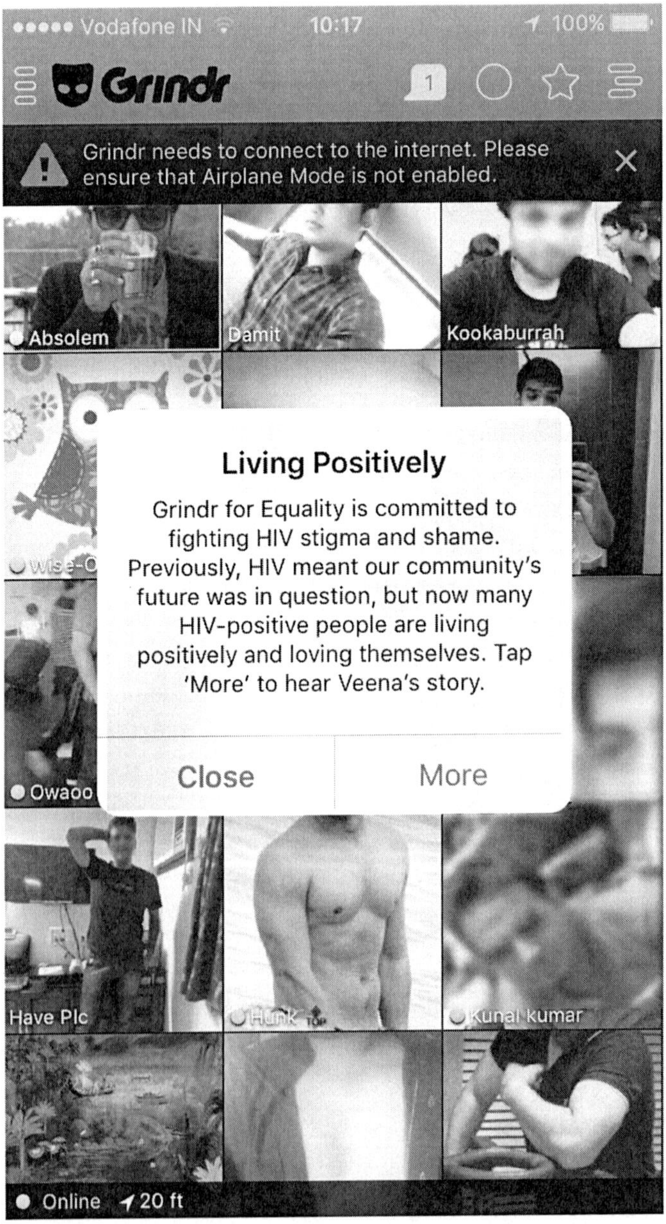

Figure 4: Grindr in Kolkata (screenshot) with pop up message about sexual health

advertise services and times, something many respondents we spoke to in this research supported. This partnership could instil trust and confidence in the services and bring together two different sectors (social media and health practitioners/advocates) with different levels of expertise.

CHAPTER 6

WAYS FORWARD

There has been a tremendous growth of digital opportunities in India- from the government run initiative aimed at bridging the digital divide to non-government agencies which are trying to use preliminary forms of digital media to connect with their service users and providing information. As our research has shown, despite the growth of 3G and 4G technology in India these have a urban bias which make it harder for people in non metropolitan areas from accessing them. Another issue is the role of social media affordance which make understanding the 'language' of some of these platforms difficult for users. There needs to be more incentivised training to overcome some of these difficulties. As 'cruising' itself is moving from the physical space of the park to the screens of our phones and laptops, peer outreach workers also need to enter these new spaces to conduct sexual health outreach. A good intervention as one respondent put it was being able to combine successful online advocacy with offline intervention.

> AH: See, there are certain websites, where if you want first is they'll give basic facts and questions, where they'll give you the basic answers; then there will be detailed sections where they'll give links where you can go on find more details. For example, if they talk about basic STIs and they say gonnorhoea, chlamydia, and they'll give links where you can have individual pages where they'll have much more detailed

> description and symptoms of those STIs, and the treatment, what should be done, how they can be treated etcetc, and those – some of the websites also have an active section where you can ask a question and somebody can respond. So that is a bit of a counselling over email or through a chat. Some of them say that from this day, from this hour to this hour, our counsellor would be sitting online for a web chat. So people can post questions and we can have this kind of a group discussion session. Some places I've heard that people can also do one-to-one web chat or even Skype chat. So that is also a possibility. And then you may have this entire doctor's desk where if there are critical medical issues, they can write to the doctor, the doctor can respond and also it can be that you have the number of a doctor and you may call up that doctor and seek an appointment. Finally, you link up with the doctors, so all this is possible provided the amount of resources available.

Two other features of a good intervention were mentioned by different respondents:

One centred around having online sexual health forums that would cater to men in general and not just MSM or other queer populations. This would have the potential to also engage men who don't necessarily identify as gay, MSM or trans* but practice male-to-male sex, something which traditional interventions have failed to do.

The second was related to obtaining government buy-in for online sexual health interventions. Whether or not government funding is used for such interventions, the increased government policing of the internet in recent times is something that has to be factored in. So while online sexual health forums are needed that provide comprehensive information to gay men, other MSM and trans* people on issues ranging from safer sex and STI/HIV treatment to sexual reassignment and protection against violence, governments are bound to act as gatekeepers of such information.

There still remain a lot of trust issues regarding new media and data capture and a majority of our research participants agreed that 'old' forms of media such as television and especially telephone helplines were still central to sexual health advocacy and knowledge dissemination. There is a need to make these much more useful with attendant funding and human resources.

CONCLUSION

To conclude we reflect and summarise the main findings from this research project, also outlining some of the limitations we encountered.

We managed to interview and invite to our four focus groups, representatives from several local sexual health organisations. Whilst there has been a growth of many small advocacy groups which provide support to queer individuals, several of these are largely underfunded. The aims of these organizations are also largely governed by the short term projects that they received and the funding aims thus having to constantly switch back and forth between their organizational aims. SAATHII still remains one of the largest HIV/AIDS sexual health charity in Eastern India though localized groups and projects such as Pehchan has allowed other regional groups to take a more centralized role in working within their communities (also see Dasgupta, 2012). The passage of the reinstatement of Section 377 by the Supreme court which criminalizes same sex activity has also led to organisations in Eastern India folding up or taking a more conservative approach.

There are only a few organisations which use social and media platforms. Whilst several of them have some sort of a social media presence largely on Facebook, these are heavily biased towards those based in the larger cities such as Kolkata. The regional and suburban organisations are yet to fully use digital media in their advocacy and reaching out programs. As our research uncovered, this was based on economic factors, lack of digital literacy and the low penetration of internet in the rural belts of West Bengal. Due to the small nature of this project and all the focus groups being mainly done in Kolkata and surrounding areas we feel we might have missed out on some of the work happening in areas such as Burdwan, Birbhum and Darjeeling areas. This will be something we will look into as we move towards applying for a larger grant to work intensively in these areas.

There are some digital media interventions that are being conducted by organisations such as SAATHII and Varta Trust. In fact, Varta Trust has been ahead of its partners by establishing new websites and Facebook forums, conducting interviews with youth groups on gender, sexuality, health and rights, and is planning workshops on community documentation. Several other digital media interventions are done by single individuals. One of our focus group participants mentioned how he uses Grindr and PlanetRomeo and has several profiles to spread sexual health awareness. There are however no 'teams' or funding to keep this sustainable on an organizational level.

This has been a successful project. Whilst the research data in terms of the number of respondents and focus groups conducted are relatively small owing to the nature of the funding and scope of the project, it has led to some useful observations and thinking how successful sexual health intervention programs might be designed for the future.

APPENDIX

FOCUS GROUP TRANSCRIPTS

Please note, there were 4 focus group discussions conducted and several informal interviews. We have only included two representative sampling here. Each focus group was run with a grouping of individuals. For example Focus Group 1 was made up of staff from SAATHII (Solidarity and Against the HIV/AIDS Infection in India); Focus Group 2 had outreach workers from different non-governmental organisations. Focus Group 3 was with youth working in the media sector and Focus Group 4 had young gender and sexuality activists from West Bengal, India. The transcripts for all focus groups and audio files for them can be requested from the research team.

FGD No. 1: SAATHII Staff Members, 14/06/16

PD : Okay, so this is the first FGD with staff of SAATHII NGO. Today is the 14th of June and the location is the SAATHII office, Kolkata. Okay, when we speak, we need to be a bit loud, but it can catch your voice. And we don't have very many ground rules, I'm sure you're experienced – please speak one at a time, not all together. So the first point is that we're talking about sexual health promotion, and what we are – what first I would like to do is - one by one just mention your name, real or imaginary, whatever, and just say something, what do you mean by sexual health promotion, in your opinion what is sexual health promotion . . . so we'll start with the left side or the right side?

AH : I'm AH and for me sexual health promotion would be, particularly for the MSM population or the transgender hijra population, would be ensuring that they have access to all prevention programmes, related to HIV and STI, and also a treatment programmes, and that in general also have access to their entire range of programmes which will help in improving their sexual health and mental health.

SJ : I'm SJ from SAATHII. In the context of sexual health for the MTH population is like getting services from the government hospitals - on sexual and reproductive health, like getting access on the condoms, lubricants and talk about their sexual activities and behaviour with the doctors, who should have the knowledge of the MTH issues, and their sexual health and rights. So, this is my perception of the sexual health.

SG : This is SG. According to me the sexual health promotion, particularly for MSM, transgender, hijra community, I generally focus on prevention and awareness - that should have a important because even we do not know about the sexual health issues – what, what - we are not fully aware about it, the community is not fully aware about it, so the awareness is much more important, playing an important role – prevention part is required along with treatment and other issues. For example, just recent of my experience, like many of my known people, many of my circle who belongs to this community – MSM, transgender, hijra – they don't have idea about the difference between the fungal infection and viral infections, different STI symptoms, and even they haven't heard about ART and PrEP. So these are some incidents I'm sharing to you know focus on the areas of sexual health promotion which we can focus on. And obviously SJ said important, very important point like health care providers' awareness and service access, high service access by the community. That's all, as of now.

PD : Okay, so . . . yeah, so, you have given me an idea of overall what do you want to see in sexual health promotion. But can we talk a little bit about the media that is used for sexual health promotion? So we can talk – we don't have to follow any order, anyone can say. What might be the media through which sexual health promotion can happen?

AH : See, traditionally for so many years that we have seen is the sexual health promotion which has worked, especially the public health interventions, whether funded by the government or other donor agencies, were traditionally focussed on the segment of the populations which are primarily lower or middle income. And this population was most visible or available or accessible in traditional places of gathering, which are like, let's say, cruising spaces or soliciting sites or sex sites. But gradually in the last decade, with the advent of internet, faster internet connections, more smart phones in more people's hands, and with the various apps, the communication has gradually changed. So in between there was an entire phase when internet was like penetrating in India – we had a number of e-forums that people were joining up and were discussing, which lead on to dating sites, which gradually now have percolated down to apps on smart phones. In between the other entire thing was about mobile networks and having this private parties, and private get-togethers through contacts or like contacting people over mobile phones. Plus in addition to all this, there is this, another area of private set-ups like house parties, where people are gathering and massage parlours also – which is also a different kind of space, which is not really accessible to health care workers – to go and do health related promotion.

PD : So you are saying that this should be the media, these are the places . . .

AH : These are all the places that current interventions are not addressing, for example, private spaces where private parties are happening, sexual or massage set-ups in massage parlours, the entire space about online dating apps, there are no health interventions going on. In some of the dating forums or dating sites, there are advice columns, or people write a post, but that has a very limited effect or impact.

SG : According to my experience, or whatever I've seen, everything is connected. Like you know we started with the traditional cruising sites and going there physically, looking for the community people according to their own timings, and those timings change very frequently, that we have seen in government programmes – the drop-out cases and the changes of time of the clients, which is very hard to track. But nowadays what happens like the face-to-face, physical cruising sites are also there, if I talk about some of the places where people go for having fun, finding partners, and most of the places I have seen nowadays people go for socializing, so in those places, even going to those places they use social networks. They use the different apps, like there are many apps which can tell you how many gay guys, how many community guys are nearby to you. So accordingly you can decide where to meet, you can decide any common soliciting place, where you both can go. So now see this physical cruising site is also actually connected with the social networking site or apps. So, this is my notice and what I think nowadays actually networks are available everywhere. We have seen the very nice nice advertisements of 4Gs in small small villages and even the desert. So if network is available everywhere, we can approach, we can introduce different apps in those places. See, the popular apps we now use in Kolkata nowadays once we didn't even heard about it, long back, few years back. But we started using, one person, then we saw oh my god, this is the thing, give me the application, give me the source of the application, we will download. So nowadays in small districts people are aware about Facebook and they check their mobile internet, they have internet packages. So if we introduce that would be a kind of a new horizon for . . .

PD : Traditionally, if I ask you to go back in time and if you can just narrate to me what kind of media have been used other than - for sexual health outreach - other than physical outreach, what are other media have been used, online, offline . . .

SJ : Like, online, in my past experience we used to provide the information through the emails or over phone, for sexual and reproductive health to MTH, to link them to the various services, and before providing or getting them linked with the services, we also worked with the health care providers or service providers so that they can also be aware about the sexual and reproductive health of, particularly of the MTH population, so that they can provide any services without any bias. And another we can use like there is a programme of – there should be a programme like the Yellow Pages. Yellow Pages provide quick information on any services, which you want. If they have any website which provide services for the cruising points, for the sexual health services, for the partners, and massage parlours, so that MTH population, because nowadays everybody is using internet, have access to the internet, they can get information through the internet and get services from the Yellow Pages. So this kind of programme will help in the intervention of the MTH populations.

PD : Okay, I will, that's good, I will come back to what is possible. First you mentioned email helpline, that was one option that used to be there or might still be there. What other options were there, other than cruising areas?

AH : If you go to the history, of course, you're sitting over here and I'm narrating your story only (laughs). See if you look at 1980s, early 90s, that entire period, you had gay groups coming up with discreet publications, where you had this post box address given, and people used to write over there. So that is an alternative to physical interactions. So people are sending letters and they're getting response through letters, then they're following up with a meeting. So my history was I was not there on the scene at that point of time, but that was what I've heard that that was one of the earliest modes of communication through pen pal columns in newspapers and through such post box addresses, sending to the support groups. This was followed by small events. Sixteen years ago when I joined that CBO called Counsel Club, they had a number of media outings. In those media outings the journalists were really friendly, so they used to publish that post box address and also the phone number. In fact, my coming to that CBO was through that post box address and calling up the newspaper, getting a number of the contact person of that organization and then gradually coming to that CBO. Later on when I joined that CBO that phone number after it got published in mainstream media, every day there were a number of calls happening. So helpline, phone helpline was the next form. Then gradually when internet had started penetrating India, and you had cyber cafes mushrooming everywhere, e-forums and online forums became the next mode of communication. After that, gradually, as internet speed started increasing, more and more sites started opening up and then you started having dating sites. And then currently you have the entire smart phone and dating apps such as Grindr and Planet Romeo. Now this – parallel to this entire communication, the entire field based or sex site or outreach site based one-to-one interactions kept on happening, but over the years, in my 16 years of work we've seen dwindling populations in the actual physical sites. So, the sites where 16 years ago I could go and find 50 people, now I may go and maximum find 10 or 12 people. So the rest of the 40 people and the new populations have migrated to other forms of communication or networking.

SG : Just to add with you AH, as you're talking about the traditional sites and the sites we have heard about long back having a lot of community crowd, I agree that decrease but different kind of physical meetings started happening. Now I know that sex parties and sex drug parties and so many parties started in different cities, even in small cities also they started organizing gay parties in different motive, there are different motives I must say, and in those parties how they communicate in that party. Nowadays the application WhatsApp, it's very easy to make a group and connect with thousands of people, not thousand obviously, that would be a high size, big size WhatsApp group. But they communicate through this social or digital media, and that is one of the ways to organize parties where they are physically meeting. That is also a cruising point for all guys. Second thing is like you're talking about phone calls and newspapers, I must say when I was growing that time the aunt agony section started giving hint of LGBT issues, and one of the areas was talking about support group in Kolkata and I came to know about SAATHII and other organizations. Adding another thing like do you know how I was outreached? I was motivated through Yahoo Messenger. That Yahoo Messenger room was like the biggest role in my life when I was 16-17, where I got to know should I go to meet community groups, will they break my confidentiality, or those things were answered nicely by the experienced people from other cities.

PD : Right, so good, I think it's a good overview of how we started and so, AH you're talking about your first, initial contact with the queer support groups must have been around early 2000s, late '90s . . .

AH : Yes . . .

PD : Right, and your information SG is about Yahoo Messenger and agony aunt columns, could be around early 2000s?

SG : Early 2000s . . .

PD : Okay, so then the next question is - fine we have dealt with what possible media were there and now are there. But now let me ask you, you personally, each one of you, how much do you use online or the internet for health related information?

SG : If it's about – see, in my field if I'm working on any particular health issue, if I need to know more about that area, or for particular some terms or everything, obviously internet, emails, e-forums, Google search, Wikipedia – these are the things we always keep doing if we do not know any area of health issues. That is one thing.

PD : So this is for your personal use, meaning for your own health treatment?

SG : No, not for own health treatment, that is for own understanding about different health care issues.

PD : In regard to your work?

SG : Yes, and knowledge building also.

AH : See, with regard to treatment if I may say – when I came on to the scene or when I started working at that point of time internet access was very limited and most people did not have access to a computer, there were very few cyber cafes which used to charge really high. So for me all my health related, safer sex, HIV, STI were through those support group Counsel Club meetings and through all those discussions. But now at this age, when I got detected with cholesterol and with sugar, for all those queries, I went to the internet and I started searching which are the sugar rich foods, which food would give you high cholesterol and all that. So I can now understand that maybe now a 16 or 17 year old, if he or she has to find out about HIV, then maybe the first thing they would be doing is search the internet, like I'm doing for my own sugar and cholesterol, they would be doing for HIV and STI – or for any query whatsoever.

SJ : I also keep searching on internet for the basic information on particular issues like HIV, or any other STIs or any further development. So this is really interesting for me to understand more about the health issues. But for my treatment part, I will prefer to visit the doctor mainly – for getting confirmation.

PD : Achha, okay can you tell me why, why would you prefer going to a doctor?

SJ : Because there are – during the searching in the internet for the particular health issues, I got a lot of information that was not . . . correct information, on that website or from the particular e-forums. So for that purpose for confirmation I would prefer to visit a doctor. Or take opinion and second opinion also I would take from another doctor, so that I can . . . certain information from the website and the doctors – so that I can connect whether the information is perfect or not.

PD : So you're triangulating . . .

SJ : Yeah.

PD : So it's a question of trust, right?

SJ : Exactly.

AH : Now my response to that is that at this age and with this much of experience, you're able to question the veracity of the information provided by the site. Now imagine a 16 year old girl or a 17 year old boy, for them that is the information, maybe that person would verify that from his or her friend, but would be hesitant to go to a doctor. But now with your experience you know that I should go to a doctor to verify the information from that source.

SJ : There are different opinions and it can vary man-to-man.

SG : This is quite strange like we have a denial in our mind. We always pick up the things that we like from internet end of the day, for example, just talking about examples, it would be much easier. If I find one pimple in my genital area and if I try to search what is that pimple about, and if I get to know about herpes and other things which is pimple issue or something like that, two reactions come – number one, either no, no, I didn't have that, just stop, close this window and go for Grindr and other sites, that is much more interesting, this disease related information which actually I can connect with my current issue, which is like something giving me depression and I'm going away from that – maybe the presentation, maybe I'm not choosing the exact site, or maybe not the right place to see the information, so it's coming as a shock for me at the first sight. For that reason what happens, either they ignore that or after that – I get calls from my friends because they think that I'm Bula Di, aajka Bula Di (laughs), so for that reason they ask me even though they have much more internet access. Maybe it is about interest, about the sites, a sex dating site – interest about the site is . . .

PD : That is fine, the competition, the health information is trying to compete with information about sexual networks, pleasure sources etc.

SG : Maybe if it's hard core health information which I'm not actually able to connect with myself I always deny, and I'm going far away from that.

AH : And to add to this, one is that yes, on the internet where health information is competing with pleasure information. On the other side that health information is portrayed in a manner which is very clinical and sometimes scary. Now as he pointed out that if a pimple - if a website is saying that this is symptom of herpes, whereas some other website will say that normally this thing happens because of heat, allergy, this and that, there will be some people who will look at the lesser serious looking explanation and will be satisfied – oh, I have just got a pimple which is from an allergy. On the other hand there will be some clients who will go paranoid with the fear that I've got herpes and they would want to run to a doctor. Now, that same information can have these two effects. But I've seen there are certain organizations, especially in the UK, where they put the information in a non-threatening manner that this maybe A, B, C, D or E – nothing to worry, you go and contact your nearest gay friendly doctor, who can help you in addressing whatever it is. So that sort of gives me an assurance that this may be serious, but it is nothing that I'm going to die of tomorrow.

PD : So, in a way the idea is to – it's difficult but it has to be interesting, it has to compete with other information that is wanting your attention, at the same time it also should not be threatening, it should not sort of put you off, or you start wondering whether even this is accurate or not, that I know that I really need to go to a doctor.

SG : Sometimes because of that they withdraw themselves.

PD : But in terms of say, we're talking about very marginalized communities like MSM, transgender, hijra – are there any advantages that online information, online health promotion, sexual health promotion might offer compared to face-to-face services or information?

SJ : Recently I got a call from . . . some client from the CBOs that the person suddenly detected HIV positive and needed like one month or two months nutritional support and shelter support, so I just requested to the shelter home that provides services like nutrition and health services to any kind of population – they are very much friendly with the PLHIV, MSM, transgender and hijra populations – so in this way I try to provide services or give the information to the MTH population so that they could not deny to them any kind of . . .

AH : See, my point was that the entire purpose this person was calling our helpline was that this person was afraid to go and talk to someone face-to-face.

SJ : Exactly.

AH : A phone line provided that anonymity of not revealing your true name, identity, location and that person would not be able to see your face, so with that anonymity there is a lot more confidence in sharing your problems. So actually in SAATHII we saw that the helpline started attracting a lot of people who had a number of medical conditions, and our counsellor had a lot of effort - had to be put in into convincing those people that yes, you need to go and visit a doctor and meet him face-to-face. So for the MTH community, that first point of contact is very necessary where somebody is able to guide, instill a trust in that person that you can go to this doctor, this doctor is gay friendly or TG friendly, this person would not judge you, would not discriminate against you and would protect your confidentiality completely. So that helpline or that email, or that dating app or whatever app has to give that trust. Then only for this community, they would be able to access health services. Or else I'm very sure that a 17, 18, 19 year old guy who realizes that he may have got some infection because of some sex with his partner, would not want to walk into Apollo or to a government hospital and ask for services.

SG : I think they know about this thing, see . . .

SJ : They can generally use helpline or email based information, without revealing any personal identity.

SG : You have asked about – the question was about what we think about this role of online, digital media in MSM, TG, hijra community – if I talk about hijra community I really have a doubt though how many – about the accessibility of any sites or any social networking sites in regular basis by them, for that reason I must say phone calls zindabad. Still now the helpline is – because unofficially, even me, AH, many people after Pehchan, one of our biggest projects under Global Fund on these community issues, so after Pehchan, even during Pehchan we kept getting calls from them, maybe he's not a client of any of the community groups, he's an individual person, doesn't know about where to get done ICTC, where to go for counselling, where to go for private HIV testing, they do not know. Even if they know, the next question would be like what is the timing, are they community friendly, these are the questions they are not getting answers from anyone, and they feel comfortable talking over phone. So, I have seen the person sitting beside me, talking with me, he didn't utter a single sentence about this issue, but before two days he called me and asked about the ICTC centres. So phone calls, I think are the concrete thing, concrete, proper helpline number circulated to everyone for any sort of support.

PD : But don't you think that - I mean this is a very good comparison, advantages and disadvantages of online information, but even the phone number to call up, can that be provided online? How will I know where to call up?

AH : That has to be – actually you need to publicize it through multiple modes because – I'll again go to the example of a 17 year old boy, who doesn't know Planet Romeo or Grindr, what he'll do is do a Google search for gay issues or something like that. So if you put this number within, let's say Planet Romeo or Grindr, this guy is never going to find this number. On the other hand, for a hijra population, who would not do a Google search, she would only come to know this number if it is on a leaflet distributed in a public event by an NGO or a CBO or during a rally or maybe some other event . . .

SG : Or maybe television advertisements . . .

AH : . . . or television ads. For some populations, for example, working class males in suburban areas who do not have so much of access to internet, maybe small posters on trains or publicity on platforms would be the only source of reaching to them.

SG : Or maybe SMS.

SJ : SMS is not possible.

AH : SMS, how will you send an SMS if you do not know the number of the person, so who will be sending the SMS to whom?

SG : Yeah, thing is like we have several SMS services, we always think like – Way2Way SMS or kind of a generic SMS for health issues, nowadays they've even started 'get ready – this is the age to have a heart attack'. I started getting this SMS . . .

AH : Okay!

SG : Go to Apollo and get your . . .

AH : Okay, those kinds of publicity which are generic, which are more targeted SMS – like 'Aapnarjounaswasthyajodi . . .'

SG : Even in Bengali! Even in Bengali, these SMS are really helpful, because I've seen many friends of mine receive these messages – this makes information accessible to everyone.

AH : So, it's another form of publicizing the number, yes I agree – yes, which is sending general SMS stating that if you have any sexual health query, then you can call up this number. But that would lead to a number of calls!

PD : Yes, that the system has to be prepared to handle those calls.

SG : Or maybe we need to think of something where we can target some of the group work with this community and we can actually – somehow I don't know, for generic messages they would be very hard to handle, even I'm thinking so. The counsellor will die receiving calls! On the other hand, I think you're right – class, location, age, community – everything will matter for publicizing such information. Different approaches will be there.

AH : I think Sahay tried that helpline, but I don't know how well publicized they were, but they had that option - if you want to talk about HIV, press this number; if you want to talk about this issue, press this number. So that kind of interactive voice response system is something possible. So, now that needs a lot of resource, money and of course the government support. You may have to get permission from TRAI and all those places. So that is doable, but that involves a lot of resource intensively.

PD : Yeah, idea will be expensive.

SG : And along with that there are certain helplines already running for different issues, and certain agony aunt sessions are also happening. So, if we can advocate with those people, after actual launching of helpline or online service, if they like if they refer our number, our online service to that particular person for particular problems . . .

PD : Okay, so, now some amount of discussion we want to do about

– since this is focussed on online communication, so can you quickly give me names of the most popular websites and apps which MSM and transgender people are using these days.

SG : Instagram, Facebook, Grindr ... Rindr or something is coming, I forgot the name; that is the better version of Grindr, it's a new thing.

PD : Just Rindr?

SG : Rindr or something, I'm not going to tell you the name now, I'll confirm and let you know...

AH : There is Tinder, where you have both straight and gay stuff also, there is Blender which is mostly for straight, Grindr which is for gay, Planet Romeo and then we're talking about Facebook and all that is already there. Now these are the most popular ones that have been used around as per my experience - there may be even more high-funda apps ...

SG : If it's about communicating with each other, if I talk about promotion, then I must talk about Youtube. First of all, like there are thousands of documentaries ...

SJ : Even Gmail chat.

Others: Yes!

SG : And WhatsApp, AH was saying, WhatsApp groups even became very popular in WhatsApp separately, and I was talking about Youtube, because small documentaries – small series, LGBT specific any information or maybe any pride walk related documentary – even students and youth are making those films and small documents and uploading on Youtube and among friends it becomes very popular ...

PD : I will just offer a counter point, because very recently I was actually looking for short films which talk about health issues, sexual health issues with young people. How do you use films to talk about these issues to young people and I was hunting on Youtube. So my counter point is this that when I compared I found some films, very interesting films, made at very low cost, and individual initiatives also, anybody can now make a film and put it up on Youtube. So there were some of them were really good, but when you compare the number of hits they receive with the pornographic films and semi-pornographic films on Youtube, there is like a difference of maybe thousand percentage points. A few thousand, 3,000, 4,000 hits for these semi-educational films; 50,000, 60,000 for soft porn films from both Bengals, on this side of the border and that side, and then such a lot of films from Bangladesh where there is such a lot of sexual assault being shown, and mainly I'm talking about straight or opposite sex films, not so much same-sex, but there are also other films where, which are mainly seen by men, but where they show two men or two women having sex. So, how do you counter that?

SG : That is a difference between – if we try to organize, or if we try to – I'll talk about two t-shirts I've seen, I have with me. One t-shirt is saying use condoms, save your life, white t-shirt printed on that in red, and with the symbol of red ribbon. Another t-shirt I got in black written condomize your tool. So I prefer to wear that (laughs). The information is similar but the presentation does matter, obviously like as we started with like approach which is competition between – you were saying AH pleasure and health – somewhere we need to negotiate and bring both of the things in a certain way that people will feel interested, and in Planet Romeo also they talk about – they have Planet Romeo Foundation for the development of community, they have HIV programmes, they promote about HIV issues, the Romeo Mother, Gay Romeo Mother comes up with a very nice attire, with very nice information which we love to read. So that is also talking about sexual health.

PD : So AH you have worked in the pleasure, pleasure principle or a pleasure collective, what was that about? What were you trying to emphasize?

AH : See, before I go on to that, I'll just talk about this global report on pleasure, which is published last year I think, now if you go through that entire report, what you'll see is that the websites, the ads they're putting up they are actually made by NGOs only. But those ads are very targeted to the gay community, where the models that are used, the amount of nudity that is being shown, everything is to bring to the mind the entire pleasure approach. So, during my entire work with pleasure, what I saw is in a massage parlour setting if I just go and say that put on a condom - that will be too boring. But if I use a, let's say, we had made this film where we are talking, showing that there is a couple, there is a massage situation happening, where the masseur is training the client on using the condom properly. Now using that material, when we had done a screening of it, a trial screening, what we saw was that people were responding quite happily. They were very interested in screening that across the state. Similarly, I saw a material from Australia, where they've used porn actors to make the entire condom demonstration, and they've taken photographs, actual colour photographs of the porn stars putting on the condom. Now that material, of course, it's private circulation only, not mass circulation, that was a material which was very liked by the community in Australia. Similarly, in UK there are people who are into BDSM. For them there is a separate website where the entire negotiating safer sex and seeking treatment, that is portrayed within the context and confines of BDSM; of how an individual who likes BDSM may want to perceive that information. So that level of customization would be required. So like you were searching Youtube, you'll get those videos but the porn videos, of course, get more ratings, so if you can implant safer sex messages within porn videos then that may work the best.

PD : Okay, you want to say something? Actually, from that last question I want to come to one of the last questions I have, is that you're saying implant sexual health information within say pleasure videos. So one concern is also this that actually in the

West, in some projects in some case studies they have seen that if there is actually that kind of information, anything to do with health within a pleasure forum is off putting for some people. So, say, in Planet Romeo or in certain other apps if you - if people know, okay, my god there is somebody here who is the health person, the condom wala, the HIV wala, as they used to say in the cruising areas, 'Wohdekho aa gaya, condom wala aa gaya!' So you know people may react negatively also to that, so what do you think about that?

AH : See, that was one of the reasons that in the '90s when in America a lot of gay men were dying of HIV and the entire porn industry were requested to show condom use in their films, there was a lot of resistance from the porn film directors and production houses because they said that then people would not buy those porn films, because they'll get put off if they see condom use. Now, it took a lot of effort in getting porn actors to wear condoms and have those – enact those sex scenes. But now with the availability of ART drugs and reduced viral loads and availability of PrEP, you have this entire bare backing scene coming on, and you can distinctly understand the entire NGO and health lobby is trying to advocate with the porn industry that please do not publicize bare back sex through your porn films. It is not working, actually because the customer demand or client demand who wants to see that porn is really high. But there are some directors who said that we'll put at least one message, so I've seen some videos where they say that 'Condom is best, and we all know porn is fantasy'. So they considered this as fantasy . . . So that was kind of a disclaimer line that came because it was a bare backing video. But there are some directors who're saying that they would not make porn without condoms. Now, there are very few directors left who are sticking to that stand, so this is an area that is difficult. Now within these forums also, in Planet Romeo or Grindr, if someone keeps talking about HIV, and very clinically, and keeps on writing then people would, of course, as SG said, they'll be blocking this person. So these messages may have to come sporadically or in a manner which doesn't intrude. So, for example, in Planet Romeo what I've seen is that there HIV messages do not pop up constantly. Sometime or the other they'll have a scroll coming up or a pop up coming up but not all the time and every time. Plus there is a dedicated button you can click on that and you can find out more information. So that's not intrusive, so people who do not want that they would not go there.

PD : Rather those who want will make the effort and find out . . . yeah, this was very useful information . . .

SG : And another thing I must say is nowadays the online shopping sites. People started buying there condoms and other accessories from there – people started searching for sex toy sites in India, so I don't know how to incorporate – and in those sites they find condoms very interesting, they try to find out different flavours, different designs or blah blahblah, so those things are actually giving them pleasure, eye pleasure or something, that they are actually sticking to that. But how to use that pleasure in the different digital or online sites where they will show their interest that we need to think . . . as you know the difference between that bidi packet type condoms, which costs one or two rupees, on the other hand the Wild Love or the other companies which have a very nice picture . . .

PD : So one other issue is that actually we're talking about how information has to be given - in a clever and sophisticated manner so that it reaches the people who really need it or who really want it. Now let's do, let's go a little bit deeper into exactly what kind of information can be given online. So normally in traditional outreach there would be information – just giving verbal information - that is one thing. The other is listening to the other person about their problems and helping them through informal and formal counselling methods – that was one activity that would often happen. The other, the third would be actual medical support, almost like treatment - so sometimes, if not exact treatment, then what needs to be done for treatment, that was also part of the work, and the fourth is, of course, either taking the person to the doctor or referring him or her to the doctor. So if we look at these four aspects of just information, of counselling, of treatment advice and actual treatment access, what can be done online? Can all four be done?

AH : See, there are certain websites, where if you want first is they'll give basic facts and questions, where they'll give you the basic answers; then there will be detailed sections where they'll give links where you can go on find more details. For example, if they talk about basic STIs and they say gonnorhoea, chlamydia, and they'll give links where you can have individual pages where they'll have much more detailed description and symptoms of those STIs, and the treatment, what should be done, how they can be treated etcetc, and those – some of the websites also have an active section where you can ask a question and somebody can respond. So that is a bit of a counselling over email or through a chat. Some of them say that from this day, from this hour to this hour, our counsellor would be sitting online for a web chat. So people can post questions and we can have this kind of a group discussion session. Some places I've heard that people can also do one-to-one web chat or even Skype chat. So that is also a possibility. And then you may have this entire doctor's desk where if there are critical medical issues, they can write to the doctor, the doctor can respond and also it can be that you have the number of a doctor and you may call up that doctor and seek an appointment. Finally, you link up with the doctors, so all this is possible provided the amount of resources available.

SJ : We used in our earlier project that we first provided information - we created the forum of good doctors and service providers, and then we provided them information on MTH population . . . so in this way we responded to our clients over phone and gradually convinced them to go to the medical doctors set-up so that they can get the technical or medical aspects from them face-to-face. Other than that we provided information over email or over phone, like whether the homosexual activities are abnormal or normal, so that kind of non-technical information we provided over email or over phone. But the technical information, like whether this is STI or not or I've got HIV infection or not, I have done safer sex but condom has burst during the – so in this case we did not take any decision over phone or email, we generally created the forum of the medical practitioners so that we can refer the client to the medical doctors and this way they can get friendly services from them.

AH : By this forum you mean panel of sensitized health care providers who all are aware of issues concerning MSM, TG and hijras . . .

SJ : Hmm, even counsellors.

PD : So that actually is a very important aspect of online dissemination - that you should not just refer anyone to any doctor - the doctor should already be sensitized and trained.

SJ : Exactly.

PD : So last two questions and then, of course, if you have any points to add, please feel free to add. One of the questions is that usually when we're talking about NGOs, so if we have to involve NGOs in online dissemination, in online sexual health outreach through whatever forum – social media or WhatsApp or chats, whatever be the various versions that you have talked about, typically who in the NGO is likely to handle these kind of activities?

SG : We need to talk about the names of the NGOs or . . . ?

PD : No, no, in any NGO that you know of or your own NGO or - I'm not asking about any specific NGO, actually NGOs in general, if anyone – if they were to start online dissemination or online outreach, who in the organization is likely to handle that activity? Decision making, of course, will be by the board or manager, director whoever, but who will handle it?

AH : Usually, in most NGOs and CBO set-ups, there is one person or the other who is sort of a counsellor or stroke documentation officer, stroke liaison person – some kind of this person is there in most NGOs. So usually NGOs tend to depute this person to handle this kind of activity. So if an NGO has certain health programmes where there is a counsellor's position, they will ask that counsellor to handle this. If they have, let's say a person who is more into outreach work or something like that, then they may ask that person to handle this position. So that is how it happens, and usually they tend to depute a junior person but many organizations prefer to have a senior, much more trained person to handle this. So it depends on the NGO structure and the number of staff it has, and the amount of staff it can spare for this. That is what as per my experience this is the situation.

PD : Yeah.

SG : The thing is like resource will matter, like it can be done by one person, if we have less resource; or it can be done by five persons, if we have good resource; even not only resource if we think that – I think it's not a work that could be done by only one person. We need one counsellor as AH said; we need one technical support – the person with knowledge of technicalities, communication and internet skills, who can actually visit and do all these experiments; we need a good graphic designer, because what I think is that we're talking about negotiations, eye catching, interesting, we need good content, we need good design, we need good visual things. For that reason I said graphic designer, but maybe not exactly graphic designer but a person who can develop these things for fast and quick posting. And also need field-based people because we're doing it sitting in the office. Somewhere, as I told you before, a gay sex party, house party, they communicate on WhatsApp and physically they go there. For that reason you need some field people also who are connecting both of the things in the initial time.

AH : PD, what I understood from your question was that maybe ABC agency has developed this entire online intervention, you need support from NGO seniors to promote and maintain that. If it is just about promoting and mentoring them, maybe this counsellor or outreach level staff is okay. But if it is talking about designing and setting it up, then as SG mentioned that you need a content designer, graphic designer – that entire host of things may be needed. And, see, for a small CBO who do not have funded projects, in that case may be their board members would be taking up this work. So maybe they will have one or two board members who are skilled or trained in this area or have an interest, so they may want to take this up.

SG : The online media we're talking about, they're many. We started with phone calls, we started with many things. So in that case I guess maybe small scale CBOs can get any of the areas where they are skilled, may be it could be a helpline only, or a very good skilled organization, technically sound organization can take up the online intervention or creating new apps, something like that, so depends on their skills and areas they want to choose.

PD : In any case some level of skill will be needed, right? It cannot be done casually perhaps. So the final question - and that might be the toughest in terms of activity at the ground level – is if, say, the national HIV programme or the national HIV response in India has to incorporate more and more online outreach, and not so much only field based outreach workers and peer educators, so, for instance, National AIDS Control Programme, so . . . what would be your advocacy thrust with them? Because my fear is that they will say, okay, in a field based outreach, we're able to validate the clients. We're able to count the numbers. How will you do that online? How will you know that your target was 1,000 and you have actually reached 1,000 separate, different people. So, if the government agencies come up with that kind of a question, how do you think that can be tackled?

AH : See (general commotion and laughter) – it's not challenging but there are issues of ethics and confidentiality - that is what is my only concern. For example, tomorrow let's say West Bengal SACS gives this grant to ABC CBO to do this work. So that CBO may set up an interactive voice response system, where all the clients calling their phone numbers get captured. So that is the one obvious thing that you have so many phone numbers coming in. Now imagine if that is not the case and they only take up phone connection from Airtel, Vodafone, whatever and people keep calling. So they may say that we will record the number because we are getting it on our mobile phones. So all these are violating ethics, but these are problematic. Now with email, if people are sending emails, they can take printouts of those emails and file them and say that see so many individual emails came. Now, the government if it really wants to play detective they can go and check the IP address of those emails. So they'll find out so many different IP addresses, but again the ethics and the morality, confidentiality questions come up. Now, if you're talking about dating apps and gay sites, there are so many profiles, the profiles have photographs - of course, there are fake profiles also, but that's the maximum you can validate. But my concern would be for this entire thing all of this violates the main core trust area of confidentiality. So that is the problem. Now one of the ways out that I would like to suggest is that instead of counting the number of people who came in touch with us, what about counting the number of people whom we successfully managed to refer to a physical service provider? So let's say 1,000 is my target, I've managed to reach to 1,200 people, I've managed to successfully refer 700 of them to may be let's say a doctor, or to a psychiatrist, or to any other health service or any other service provider. So that would be a physical point of contact, which validates my 700 clients I've reached.

PD : But the immediate question that comes to mind is that how many referrals will actually be successful?

AH : Well, our Pehchan experience says around 45%.

PD : Of people you refer or who will go without being accompanied?

AH : Oh okay, no, no, that data (general commotion and laughter)...

SG : That would require online intervention or process. See, we need to actually be little bit of, like we need to make it bit relaxed from the traditional way of validations and the successful referrals. In those cases you know how we know one video got much popularity – number of hits, number of likes, number of comments, something like that. If we focus on quality through online - to start with how many people are responding, how many hits are there, how many people are actually coming up with feedback. Or maybe we may have an anonymous feedback sheet online which could be signed or may be could be marked by people, only marked! So there can be a love sign, a tick mark, smileys which show you whether I liked it or not. The referrals, after making referrals, if you liked it, fine smile, if you didn't like it ... counting them and getting the quantity, I was just thinking.

AH : Imagine a donor like NACO giving you money and asking for hard core data!

SJ : But there is a problem also in the NACO programme, national HIV/AIDS programme also, they're not providing sufficient money to the outreach worker. So that we can hire experienced and skilled outreach workers, and outreach workers are not providing sufficient information to the clients and are not able to motivate them to access the services, and that is the reason we are not getting refer-backs successfully, what I've referred, the number I've referred for the services. This is a challenging area and ...

SG : And even another hurdle we will have to face when they will go with this kind of pleasure and very much entertaining source of information to NACO, I don't know how much would be accepted or not, I really have a doubt . . . because the next thing was from my side like some of the interesting magazines, that is also media, works a lot for giving information and getting a white page of leaflet talking about ICTC would be very boring for me. I'll get a very nice coloured magazine with information and even online. There are many small groups working for rights, gay rights issues in West Bengal, in Kolkata. Another group if I create people will join. I can make it sure I have 1,000 people in Facebook, 500 of them will join that group. So I need to entertain, put something everyday which they can read. If I say I'm sad, no one will visit and no one will comment or no one will click on the like button. But if I say something interesting, so those things need, you know, that kind of approval and support.

SJ : Like I used to – in the case of MTH population, those who suspected for the HIV infection, so this is my personal experience, and I have created connections with a few of the ICTC counsellors. And we generally talk about the sexual and reproductive health of the general population as well as the MTH population. They are also very friendly about the MTH population. So we generally used to refer to that kind of sensitive person, that particular counsellor, so that they can make them understand that what they have done, and what they have, you know, getting infection or whatever activity they've done, so while talking to the counsellor they get pleasure that what they have done is not a guilt. In this way they go for the further treatment process also successfully. And this is very rare activities which we have done under the Global Fund programme or national programme due to the target and achievement . . .

PD : That means quality of service provider ultimately matters if the referrals have to succeed.

SJ : Exactly, exactly . . .

PD : Word of mouth will spread, people will trust, okay going to such a doctor is really useful. So that means online work has to be complemented very well with actual offline services, because you can't provide everything online. So last round, any other thought or suggestion which you would like to add?

AH : Now, if at the end of this research if there are any recommendations for donor agencies about inclusion of online approaches within the traditional modes of outreach work, this point would be a point of concern about validating the data. So we need to be very careful how . . . the research team formulates that sentence, and maybe we have to put this entire disclaimer that this approach would work, of course, there is enough evidence that this would work, but validating that we have to be much more innovative. So the parameters of validation, maybe the definition of indicators, means of verification - all of these have to be very innovatively thought of. So you cannot just take up the indicators of an onsite outreach model and just put them on an online model.

SG : And along with innovation I would add another issue that is about being open. Like, they are approaching a new thing which is different from traditional outreach. So they need to be open about it, bit relaxed about it and give it time. Otherwise like if in first chance people get demotivated working on this online thing, they will not actually go far. And another thing is that offline, the traditional outreach is also important. People are end of the day meeting physically and they are gathering, they need social spaces, they need to gather and we need to keep it in mind, so somewhere – where the connection of online and offline that we need to think and for different levels of people.

AH : And thank you SG for pointing that out, because PD, that is an area that in traditional TI or any NGO funded programmes, outreach workers are not encouraged to go to such private parties or to let's say a massage parlour or to a discreet sex party happening. So maybe - but those are the places where the most amount of vulnerable, risky sex is happening, most need of condoms is there and that is where the outreach workers are not present. So maybe traditional intervention projects would also have to keep in mind that now our populations have migrated on to other places.

PD : That challenge is already there . . . SJ, anything?

SJ : No.

PD : Okay, so thanks a lot. This was quite a lot of information as you can see my notes (laughs) – they've filled up all the pages. And if there is need for any more clarifications, I will again get in touch. And it might happen that later when my co-researchers are here in Calcutta, they might want to talk to you individually for more details – because this is the first FGD, so more questions might come out of this.

FGD No. 4: Young Gender and Sexuality Activists, 7/08/16

RDG: Let's begin with brief introductions . . .

RB : I'm right now doing my Masters from Calcutta University in journalism and mass communication. Apart from this I have been working on gender based issues, breaking gender stereotypes, and I try to use film as a medium. I have made one film portraying various issues of stereotypes – not just related to the LGBT community, but overall gender based stereotypes.

AVD : Well, I started working on sexuality and gender – though that's not my field of work – I did my engineering from IIT and then I gave my Masters and then I moved to Canada for my Ph.D., but right now I'm like – I think I'm changing my career from software to something more human rights because I have been working on sexuality and gender based issues for last eight years. I worked for ILGA and Pan Africa ILGA, and then I used to work for ARC International which is based in Switzerland.

So yeah like my main goal is just to have an equal world – it sounds right now pretty far-fetched, but yeah it's my goal I'm looking forward to – I came back to India last year and all I'm trying to do is to have a survey in India based on violence and discrimination because – you must be aware that there was like a resolution passed in the United Nations Human Rights Council like last month on having an independent expert – so I was working with the people who are actually in touch with United Nations, and I think we must have a survey on how violence and discrimination are being unleashed on LGBT, especially transgender and sometimes it silences the voices of gay men and lesbian women as well, so yeah that's my goal for next six months; and then I might be doing my Ph.D. once again, on this particular issue.

PB : Okay and you want to do the Ph.D. here in India or . . .

AVD : I might have to go abroad because - I would love to be in India and work, but the government in India right now sounds terrible. They've come out with some outrageous bills, though they're talking about protection of transgender people's rights. But if you look at the bill, that's not protection, that's outrageously humiliating. So I might be going abroad – I was working towards you know like reaching out to the Indian stakeholders. The response I get is not satisfactory. So I might have to go abroad, like somewhere maybe States or Canada or UK, or like Brazil – I was in Brazil for six months and they do amazing work in the field of . . . I will figure it out eventually. That's all.

RDG: Okay, so I think one of the things I want to start off this focus group with is to actually see – because it's about sexual health promotion so we're talking about how we can use social media and digital media for promoting different kinds – you know sexual health behaviours. So I wanted to kind of start by asking what you understand by sexual health promotion, have you seen health promotion, what kind of health promotion has actually caught your eyes the most in India. So, for example, I remember quite a few years – maybe 8 or 9 years ago – there was Bula Di . . .

AVD : I was thinking about it . . . (general laughter).

RDG: So is there similar anything that really caught your eyes and that you remember – it doesn't have to be something to do with MSM or gay men but anything that you thought worked . . .

RB : When I was in school life, this Bula Di thing was going on. I was maybe 7 or 8, and at that time I did not have an idea actually what is a condom, and they used to distribute condoms around my school and in the neighbourhood around my school, so I just got caught up and like there were people who just took it for fun to see what it is, and that was the first time that I saw a condom. So after that I started – I asked my parents why they are doing this, why they are distributing, so that was the first idea, I had any idea like people talking about sexual health, so – but that was – I think that was effective at some point, but I think that really did not have much outreach, though the Bula Di campaign was really accepted throughout the country, but because of its like very – it was not much layered and it had lot to say but it was not at all vulgar, which was much fit for the Indian audience, so I think that I liked that. But the thing that they reached out for condoms that really did not – like people did not have the idea that, like most people still think that condom is just used as contraception. So many gay men avoid condoms because they really, I mean I have come across people who say that we don't get pregnant, so the idea of sexual health is still much limited. This distribution of condoms was – in fact, it had a limited purpose and limited outreach, so I felt that at that point. So right now there are lot of people, like since after coming in touch with various NGOs who work with men having sex with men and trans women, so there I understood, there I saw that they are working at different levels distributing condoms, but the sex workers, the trans sex workers, they hardly use condoms. The people I have met, the interviews I have seen, for the sake of their profession they think that using condoms would stigmatize them, like their customers would think that they are diseased, or they would rather not use it because the customer would not be satisfied – they would say that using condoms would not be satisfactory enough, and they don't have the trans sex workers, I mean the hijra community who does sex work – they don't have this proper set-up, which I mean the women sex workers have in various places, in different pockets of Kolkata where it is easy to reach there and make them understand what is actually happening. I mean it is easier to educate, but here the location per se is difficult and you hardly get to know where this is happening . . . if you go from Esplanade to Park Street and take this car you'll see trans women sex working there, but people hardly know about it – only a few people of the community and activists and people who are interested in that go there. And so the outreach is very limited, I mean it is very important, like there is this process, there are various NGOs going, having sessions and workshops with people, workshops with women talking about sexual health and they are understanding the thing, this thing is very limited, because they have their own culture – this sex work is a side business and apart from that they have this own crisis of identity and the whole pressure on them for being different, for choosing something different as a profession and for themselves being different. So it becomes very difficult for us, for everyone who is working on this kind of issues to make them understand, I meant to open a different chapter – I mean talk about sexual health in a different way. Like when you talk to a queer person or a trans woman – I'm talking about trans women here because I have more interactions with them – so when you talk to them – I think you know the terms kothi, dhurani or trans women – like when we are talking to them it is more about their own conflicts. When we go to their sexual health, that thing gets diluted because there are so many other things with them. So there should be a very different section or part of any workshop that is being conducted on sexual health and health issues. Like not just sexual health – I mean this can be taken as sexual health, I'm not just talking about STDs and STIs; there are kothis and dhuranis who take I-pills and other contraception pills as unprescribed hormones, so I think this also comes under sexual health. So they don't know and they think that – and when you talk about then the counselling goes on at mental levels and the psychologist . . .

RDG: So are you saying that there is counselling that is happening, but there is no promotion, that they don't know?

RB : First they don't know the – I mean we know, we living in this metropolitan city have a lot of outreach, but people outside this place, in the various pockets of Bengal, they hardly know – they work in the fields in the morning, they dress up in the night and they enjoy their life and they have sex. So it is very difficult – and for them it is very difficult to find a platform to express their own identity, and the work that has been happening, I mean that is focussed on that section and I think it is very much needed, but the sexual health part – that is still much, it is very much into the package but it is not very much concrete. When you go and talk to a person about sexual health, a person of a different gender identity, people first start talking about their various layers of struggle that they have been going through since their childhood, but when it comes to sexual health it means a very – a wholesome package, I think it means that a person needs to go through a journey, and one needs to make that person understand how sexual health is important. And it is much more important for them, because the accessibility of trans women and gay men indulge in sexual activity because of freeness, I mean the freeness is much more, sexual indulging is much more than the hetero-normative or the heterosexual society as we see. So for them

I think – all of us need to make them understand how sexual health is important. There are various topics, issues and focus on the social media, there are people talking about – like there is this foreign ad on condoms, like Durex has put up a separate brand for gay men, condoms for gay men, they are promoting that. I think there is a need for a campaign like Bula Di which happened years back. Regarding the whole idea of sexual health, a separate campaign for people – and that should include people of alternate sexualities, it should focus on them, like Bula Di had an outreach and people, at least for the sake of unsafe pregnancies and unwanted pregnancies they started using condoms. But another campaign is needed that will reach the grass roots and will also include alternate sexualities, that will be great.

AVD : Yeah, I do agree with you . . . Years ago when I was in Bangalore, couple of us, we were doing a survey, a small survey within the so called LGBTIAQ+ community, and then we had 20 young gay men, 17 were actually tested and they had no idea, they didn't know before going ahead with the test, they had no idea that they were infected by HIV. A second survey was conducted in the year of 2002-03, there was a group called Alternative Law Forum based in Bangalore and they had done a survey especially with hijras and kothis in Bangalore. They talked about various issues; they talked about the violence, what kind of discrimination they face. So one of the aspects of that study was the sexual health of those hijras and kothis in Bangalore, and what we saw is like they were not aware at all that even when, you know like, a hijra or a kothi individual, I mean for them using condoms was – they were like why do we use it, because we cannot be pregnant, so there was no question of using it. So what I feel is like that our campaign which has been started by the government or various other stakeholders, the main idea might have been that okay, you should be using condoms because you don't want to be pregnant, but essentially what happened was that we excluded the alternate sexuality people, meaning people with different gender identities and different sexual orientations. It was again we constructed a man-woman gender binary thing, and I mean like as if not having pregnancy is the only thing you should be using condoms for. So we haven't really talked about sexual health. I mean the sexual health programme has been initiated by various NGOs who actually were working at the very grass root levels. They understood how important that is because right now like for me since I know a little bit about HIV and AIDS and all this stuff, I understand that being infected is not the end of the world, but for many that's not the case, because they have absolutely no idea, so for them being infected means the end of the world. So this kind of programmes have to be done and, I feel that we have progressed a lot in the last five or six years because of the widespread media coverage and awareness campaigns done by individuals or groups or various NGOs. So yes, we're actually progressing but the pace is – until and unless we have a strong back-up from the government, how much can an NGO or an individual do? They cannot reach 1.2 billion people, that's completely funny if you ask me to reach 1.2 billion people, but if we have government backing that will be helpful for all of us.

PB : So the question that comes to my mind is that how much investment has been made into sexual health projects and quite basic messages like condom use as well in the last decade or two, and yet somehow you're both indicating that really a lot of people have been doing projects to establish a relationship between condoms and HIV, or sexual risk . . . despite all that work and investment, there is still a huge gap.

RB : I think there is a gap, and when you go to this ICTC thing like for check-up and all that, the way they behave is terrible, and if you do not belong to the mainstream, and if you belong to someone from alternative sexuality, they will behave like as if you are something else and untouchable, and you have HIV already. So it's very frightening and they would ask unnecessary questions like they would try to emphasize – if it's a kothi or dhurani identity and if they get it, and they would try to know that whether you have slept with a man and that is the main thing that becomes more important for them. Whether you have had sexual intercourse or not that they ask later, you slept with a man, and they behave as if that is the only way you can get it, and they don't even talk about blood transfusion and other risks . . .

PB : This becomes an interesting kind of conflation . . .

RB : And they even say that you can – like I have a friend who said that right after 377 was put off, that thing was again criminalized, this lady on the opposite side said that they can deny treatment if you have slept with a man.

RDG: And I think this becomes quite interesting like post-2013 how has things changed, do you think people are now much more unlikely to go because of that, because they will be asked how do you, why do you think you got a sexual disease, it is because you've slept with a man, may be that is also something that is keeping a lot of gay men . . .

RB : Man or woman it doesn't matter, why would the other person, why would the counsellor, she's saying she's a counsellor, she's supposed to behave like one and make people comfortable. People coming with such risks, like they're already frightened - what if I have HIV, and if you're like scaring the hell out of them, so why would they come for the next time?

AVD : But you know like I remember one incident in 2009, when I thought I had HIV and I was frightened – I had no idea and simply was not aware about it, and I went to a government hospital in Bangalore, I was in Bangalore, and then I was lucky I don't know why, the doctors and the counsellors were absolutely empathetic and compassionate. They said like you can sleep with man, woman, it doesn't really matter. But that really happened actually after the 2009 Delhi High Court verdict. So they talked about it, they said sit down, have a seat and that's the first time I was treated by a government official, and I was like 'Oh vow!' I do not know whether this is about verdict or not, but I sometimes believe that people, I mean whom you're going to, it also depends upon that, if you do belong to a very stereotypical man-woman gender binary construct and family, you know like it's most unlikely that you will be compassionate towards those who are being affected. I'm not too sure but I've seen a varied range of doctors, I've talked to varied range of government officials who have a varied range of opinions from extremely positive to extremely negative. So you know like it's a spectrum of opinions, that's what I've understood. But again what I said was like you don't have any framework. I mean the government does say that these are the rules that you have to follow, but they don't implement it and there's absolutely no punishment if a government official is not following those norms. So I think that's one of the reasons that government officials can actually behave in a very negative way. Because many governments, many state governments have very inclusive health policies, which is nice. I know about Tamil Nadu and Karnataka; they have very inclusive health norms. Sometimes they follow, sometimes they don't – I don't know why. So that could be . . .

RDG: And it's very interesting because – just moving to the next section, but you've yourself mentioned about you know awareness campaigns that have been launched on social media by NGOs. Can you tell me a little bit about these campaigns maybe? So the next question was basically trying to ask you if you have ever you know actually used the internet to look up information about sexual health, and if so, what kind of sites you have looked at. But before we move on to that, because you brought that point up about these awareness campaigns by NGOs using social media, like what was the style, what did they do?

AVD : It's really interesting how it works and exactly the way NGOs reach out to people who are bit vulnerable. So again when I was in Bangalore, I was not a part of this Calcutta LGBT movement because I was from, I was born and brought up in Bangalore. So anyway, what we thought when we first saw that the situation was actually going out of our hands because people were falling sick and people had no idea what to do, so we're already minuscule minority if you know the term, but you do not want to lose more number of people. So what we thought was like most of the gay men, I'm talking about gay men, not transgender women or transgender men here, they used social networking for hooking up, for dating, finding another sexual partner, there were websites like Planet Romeo, though Grindr wasn't there in those times . . .

RB : There was Mingle too.

RDG: So which year was this?

AVD : It was in 2009 . . . so we started having a profile on every group which was talking about people who were looking for sexual partners.

RDG: So were these profiles of the organizations?

AVD : Individuals, we were not part of NGOs but we were a bunch of individuals who thought that this could be done. And so we all had our work because that time I was doing my Masters. Anyway, so whoever had time, we had profiles on those groups. We used to have multiple profiles – I had 40 profiles for 40 different groups and I had to maintain all those profiles, and my job was to monitor whoever is seeking sexual partners, and then I would be going ahead and liking it first and then commenting there 'I'm sure that you're using condoms'. So this is the way we started doing it, and then we got a bit of response, and then you know like after this 2009 Delhi verdict, things were starting a little bit in a nicer way actually – that people were talking more about their sexual orientation, people were becoming open about it, people were defying stigma, and talking about all the stuff. So many, many pages in India based on LGBT rights, so called LGBT rights had been popped up, and we found it's the absolutely best platform to reach out to people. So as I said we started having profiles, then after two years we first conducted our – the first HIV, free HIV test only for gay men and transgender like sex workers. That's the way we reached out to people and after 2013 Supreme Court verdict, it happened, when you give people freedom and when you snatch the freedom away from them, they become more vocal. We saw I mean like if we saw profiles of 4,000 people till 2013 that verdict, suddenly we saw a profile of 8,000 because more people started talking about it, more people felt this is the time when we should talk about it. So that's the way we reached out, and then we had Grindr, and then we had Planet Romeo where we have profiles of you know like, I have a profile on Planet Romeo, the name of the profile is Sexual Health and talks about why we should be using condoms. So this is the way we reached out to people – I left India in 2012, but then the campaign actually was because all our idea was to move on to and make people aware, more and more people aware. So at the end of 2014, the data was – we reached out to – in Bangalore, I'm talking about only Bangalore – there are other cities which are doing the same thing – in Bangalore we reached out to at least 7,500 gay men and we told them about - at least now they know what HIV is all about and how to prevent it, not – well sometimes we all become horny but that doesn't mean that you can go mad and take risks, so yes, I mean like that's a nice way to reach out to people, that's what I felt, that other NGOs like PD will be knowing something in Calcutta, the other NGOs in the rural areas of West Bengal, in Tamil Nadu, in other states they have been doing the same, so yes, we reached out to many people, and so we have saved lot of lives so far . . .

RB : Yeah, the thing is that there has been a lot of outreach, when in 2009 I was in class 9, there was this sudden – like I was not much aware about myself, I was in my high school, and then I saw suddenly – I had heard about the terms homosexuality, gay men, but then suddenly I saw that newspapers and TV were all covering gay rights, because that decriminalization happened, and again by 2013 I was in my college and I knew everything about myself, and everywhere what is happening – so that time it was taken away, so throughout this I really agree with him that there has been huge outreach, various NGOs they talk about HIV - in Bengal every active NGO wherever you go, they talk about sexual health, use of condoms, but the thing is that these detailed sites and the people who are in there in India, in Calcutta, and the people who are not there, I'm seeing like there are profiles, a lot of profiles who are not openly gay or bisexual, they are married men, they are people who do not actually say that they are bisexual, gay, and they do not – and they do not, they have this, they just say that they have sex with men, men having sex with men, but they deny it – like there is a whole society full of people who indulge in sexual activities like this and this whole thing, like having random sex and not just transgender sex workers, there are gay men who have sex just to have pocket money, just to earn an extra bit. So they are there, this condom thing is there, they know everything, they know that they have to use a condom, but this very idea, this very fear that you can get HIV or other STIs and this fatal health risk that you have, I mean this is not just about knowing that you can have HIV and about using condoms, it's about that very sensitization that you should have that this risk, this is something very dangerous, this is something really you need to know and avoid.

RDG: So if someone came up to you and asked you like okay I'm worried about this, what would you say, are there websites or something you would recommend to them?

RB : You see there are – like there is Amitie' Trust, like every NGO who talks about sexuality, alternate sexuality, and even women oriented organizations, they are talking about sexual health and alternate sexualities, and they refer them to various places. The thing is it's not just about knowing HIV issues, condoms and the risks, but it is more important to know that this is just not a disease, it is something to do with the whole – it is something also to do with human interest, like you have to understand that it is not just sexual health, it is also something to do with your place in society. Everything changes, and this fear does not really happen until the victims they suffer, but before that I mean the precautions, and the whole trauma that they go through – they really, I mean there is this whole gap between this victim, there are people who are outreaching and talking about sexual health, and people going to the victim and helping them, and there are certain pockets where you talk about sexual health; there are certain people who knows that these are the risks and there are the whole crowds who know these are the risks, but there is this huge gap between the trauma that the victim suffers and the person who is going to have unsafe sex right now . . .

PB : In a way you are pushing us to think what we mean about sexual health . . . so, in one way we can think of sexual health in a very linear sort of safer sex and condom use, and I think you're both pointing to sexual health related well being, mental health, discrimination, rights and so on and so forth, and I just wondered in your encounters with other people . . . do you still feel that the main messages you are encountering are very linear?

RB : I sometimes still feel so, because it is not just about the section of people who say that they are the LGBTIQ people. But there is this whole lot of people, who just do not identify themselves with the community, but they have sex with men, they go to the people, the trans, the pockets where hijra women are having sex. So these are the places that are not really tapped. Some years back when I did not, I mean when I was not much stable and I was going through a very difficult phase, I had been intimate with a lot of people. So there I had known people of various ranges, people from various sections of society, various layers, they are from different set-ups. Some are married, some are girl friends, some just identify themselves as gay but do not know what is exactly the whole thing about being gay, and some people do not – they just think that this is just about sex, there are bisexual people who think that having sex with men and being romantic with women is being bisexual. So there are a lot of people who have various layers of misconceptions. So when I am going to have sex with a person, right now I'm very much conscious about myself, and who do I go to bed with, but then . . .

RDG: So you mentioned these misconceptions and about providing the right information, I would like to bring you guys back to thinking about bit more about the digital and the social media side of things and kind of think like would there be websites you would ask them to look at, would there be like would you ask them to check-up Facebook . . .

RB : There are no specific websites you can go through, it's just that like risks with anal sex and HIV and you can just . . .

RDG: How would you know that something is a good site, like would there be something, you know instead of just Googling . . .

RB : It is definitely Google – actually I have not personally found apart from certain sites of NGOs which cater to some limited mass, there are no specific websites who talk about sexual health or what is sexuality, specifically alternate sexuality, then it has to be . . .

AVD : So far the websites and groups, the mainstream groups, groups who talk about sexual health they are not really open towards sexual diversity. They talk from the construct of man and woman, or a construct of heteronormativity. But there are mainstream media, mainstream online media, especially mainstream online media, not the mainstream media houses, they are actually slowly opening up towards these alternative genders and sexualities. There are online media like Youth Ki Awaaz – I wrote a few articles for them. They have a whole, I mean looking at it from a very mature perspective having a completely different section for LGBTQI+ people is something humiliating to me. I mean why would you have a separate blog for LGBTQI people, that means you think that we are not mainstream, but again we have to think from the Indian perspective that we are just learning right now how to accept it, and any online media who are run by so called mainstream heteronormative set-ups actually opening up and for LGBTQI rights is something that sounds wonderful to me and I would surely want to use it as much as I can. So there are groups as you said, if you are part of LGBTQI population, and if you are a part of what's going on around you, there are several groups which have, like Kolkata has several Facebook online groups, at the same time Bangalore has, Bombay has different groups and they literally always talk about sexual health. Not only that, sometimes those groups who meet offline, just to take forward the dialogue from the online space to the offline space, they too have some sort of agenda, like we're going to talk about HIV and the risks and the various steps we can take if we're infected. So yes, there are within the LGBT space, using social media or digital media is quite helpful . . .

RDG: And what kind of social media do you think gay men, trans men, trans women are using in India these days? Like where do you think people are there now?

RB : Social media as in dating sites?

RDG: It could be anything . . .

AVD : Facebook would be one of them; I guess that it is one of the most popular sites, though it has its loopholes . . . Grindr for dating, yes . . .

RB : There's Pink Cupid for lesbians I think.

PB : The sites you're talking about, I'm not sure if Grindr and others, do they have any links or integrated messages around sexual health in these sites?

RB : Yes, there are but people mostly avoid them.

PB : But people avoid them?

RB : They just go for hook-ups. That is what I was saying – I was saying that there is this diversity of people, so when I go and have sex with that person, so that person is not using a condom and when I refer – I'm diverting a bit – like there are pages in my Facebook where anything that starts with Q and L I like it. Because I identify with queer or LGBT, I identify myself with T . . . I identify myself with that community so I like it. But there is this forum like the Logical Indian, like the Speaking Tree and there are various other mainstream blog which every user likes. So they don't talk about such issues, even if they talk about sex education it is limited to the men and women binary . . .

AVD : Yeah, actually . . . (general agreement)

RB : So when I'm meeting a person, who doesn't identify with the LGBTQI community but is having sex with me, so I cannot ask him to – he would be much inhibited to hear the word G, T, Q – 'I'm not GQTB, I'm something else, I'm straight!'

AVD : I'm straight and having sex with a man . . .

RB : Okay, that is not my concern, that is a whole different topic, I have to make him go through years of counselling to make him accept himself, but the immediate need is that I have to make him understand what is sexual health, there are sexual risks involved and how that is important. And for that I have to refer him to such mainstream blogs like the Logical Indian or the Speaking Tree and there are various other places like he can go to – so I can say 'Didn't you see that blog, didn't you see the link that came up?' So that is more important, that is why I started, but there are no such platforms as such, they hardly talk about sexual health . . . even Facebook doesn't talk about sexual health.

RDG: So for example, you know the NGOs, I think all of you have been mentioning that the role of NGOs seems to be quite important in sending out sexual health promotion messages. So you have organizations like SAATHII,Vartaetc which have a Facebook presence . . .

AVD : Very strong Facebook presence . . .

RDG: Very strong presence, but most gay men are not going to Facebook to hook up. They're going to Grindr or Planet Romeo to hook up. Do you think there is any NGO presence or any kind of sexual health queer workers presence required there, and if so how would it look like?

RB : I think NGOs have a role of not just talking about sexual health to specific communities - it needs to be more diverse. Like there should be separate work going on making people understand that being LGBTQI is not wrong, but apart from that there should be a different campaign going on which would just talk about sexual health and involve everything in it, I mean men having sex with men, men having sex with women, anal sex, vaginal sex, all kinds of sex . . . so they should talk about every kind of sex, not just one kind of sex. People just – people should make it more visible. Even the Bula Di campaign did not have sexual health - I mean they did not cover the sexual health of gay men and people of alternate sexualities. The ads just showed men and women. So there should be mainstream visibility of such things. There is this visibility of the LGBTQI community, there are certain ads, there is this bogus serial going on putting out wrong ideas about what is being transgender, so there are lot of things happening – there is this serial on 'Colours' – they show that 20 years later the girl thought, I mean the girl she's a biological cisgender girl but she is shown to be transgender 20 years later, but actually what they mean is that she is intersex. And for 20 years the kinner community –

anyway that is very funny! So there are certain things happening, but they are very much separate from each other. I mean if you talk about LGBT there is this label that this is queer and only queer people are looking up to it. When you put up a label it becomes difficult for everyone to accept it, everyone doesn't identify with that label. I mean accepting yourself is different, that's a different process. But if you talk about sexual health and general health, then you cannot use a label, you have to show everything without a label. And this is something lacking in every media. Yeah, social media I definitely think that it is the most modern and evolving form of media and everyone should use it. Everyone uses it and there is a lot of scope of talking about these issues and various blogs like they're talking about these, but when you talk about an LGBTQI blog only the LGBTQI people are liking and LGBTQI people are sharing it, other people are just overlooking it. There are women, women are known to be natural allies, they're looking, they're going through those websites, but men, it is more important for men but there is very less involvement of men in such things, because men think when you get attached with the GT community, your masculinity would be questioned, and they would just not like such a page.

RDG: Right, but also you know that this is still about mainstream social media, but now I'm more interested in the gay websites or queer websites like Planet Romeo, Grindr, Gay Romeo, whatever and if there is any presence there?

AVD : About Grindr, I'm not bit active on those websites, but I've seen sometimes that some messages popped up all of a suddenly like on Grindr, and you know like talking about advocating sexual health and other stuff, but so far no, the answer would be no. I haven't seen much presence of advocacy.

RDG: Would you like to see something, let's say, maybe like a local NGO actually having a profile on Grindr?

AVD : Actually that is exactly what we did - we had a profile on

Grindr . . .

RDG: You said about such a profile.

PB : So what you had set up was you and some friends having profiles which had sexual health messages . . .

AVD : Actually, I can still show you the profiles, if I have it here . . .

RDG: Sure.

AVD : I think I deleted all those applications, but I might have something . . . so yes, what essentially we did was having profiles on Planet Romeo because that time that was the only website maybe for us, but I have . . .

RDG: Maybe you could also take the screen grab of it and send it to us.

AVD : I can do that, but I can also show it to you at this moment . . .

PD : You could keep looking for it, but in the meantime we can continue . . . (general agreement).

PB : The present issue, I think both of you pointed to it one way or another, is that – I know in some ways it is kind of sexual health promotion which presumes some rational choices – you know this is risky therefore don't do it, okay but there's a whole kind of way in which when one is online, looking for sexual partners . . . we're just making choices for other kinds of reasons, and that sort of in a way sexual risk is not always part of sexual desire, you know what I mean, sometimes you're not coming from that perspective or wavelength, and I wonder what we do with that in our personal interactions, but what we might also do with those kinds of motives online, what kind of messages, what kind of platforms might be useful?

RB : There's this one option like you have safe sex or not, like Grindr and PR and every dating site, that this is in your profile . . . but every person writes safe sex doesn't indulge in safe sex. I don't have a condom, I don't use condoms, I mean it's like they're using the same condom 15 times, so that is what is one is focussing on. It's not just about Grindr or certain sites – talking about sexual health on such sites won't just help because people just overlook such messages there, and most people there just go to have their sexual release, and people who just look for love in those sites are avoided. So how can you expect that people who – there is this message coming up on sexual health, people would just become irritated.

RDG: Right, right . . .

RB : And people would just like to avoid it, and there's this first message that comes up in Grindr as soon as you open the website, I mean when you're registering for the website, like they would give up a message disclaimer on sexual health and everything, people just skip that ad and go to the next – I mean that happens everywhere, it cannot happen like that. You have to make it more visible, more mainstream, and I'm using the word mainstream – and I think Facebook has all these kind of applications like this refresh your memories after one year, see this, see that – I mean they should have something like that too, such applications too – they are celebrating this . . . convening this, convening that and they are being happy on those issues, but they are just not talking about sexual health, not even sexual health of men and women, which is very important.

PD : Just one thought coming to mind is that see, consider the fact when you are going to a mall for shopping and perhaps you have a pre-fixed agenda, you have a shopping list that these are the things you want to buy, but there are a whole lot of other things lying around, everybody all those products are screaming for your attention and then you buy a few things almost always – impulse buying is what we call . . .

RB : I don't!

PD : You don't . . . (laughter) . . . but do you think that would work, say, in Grindr or Planet Romeo?

RB : That works to a certain extent actually . . .

PD : I'm saying that let that information be there . . .

RB : No, so there is this package of Dove, and you say oh my god, the sunscreen is free, so you just look at it definitely, but about the money . . .

PD : Do you think this logic would work for sexual health messages on Grindr?

RB : That works to a certain extent 20% that this hypodermic needle theory you have in communication, like slowly it will have the effect and you see the same thing over and over and over again . . .

AVD : Yes, this is the profile I had . . . on Planet Romeo and we have changed the name in the last one year, but then after few – four-five aspects we have that HIV related stuff, and then we have a website for gay men where only HIV positive people should be allowed to open their profiles on the dating websites.

RDG: Fabulous, can you send me a picture of this, a screen grab . . .

AVD : Sure, I can do that.

RDG: Yeah, what you're saying is very . . .

PD : Yeah, that is one thought, and the other is that when you're talking about – I missed part of the conversation – but we were also talking about the other sexual health programmes which have been run or were running through Bula Di, in all this there was a lot of government investment. Right? And that investment was along certain lines. The initial years there was a lot of confusion but then budgets were worked out, budget lines were worked out and justified by government departments to their higher ups and all of that. So what could be the approach if we were to talk to the government to include online campaigns . . .

RB : I don't know about the government, but the corporates have this social responsibility and the corporates these days are trying to be queer friendly.

AVD : No, what PD was asking was . . .

PD : Yeah, because the whole thing is that the corporates might also step in only when they see a policy because they may not want to antagonize the government. So how do you convince the government to take up online campaigns because many such efforts have been made and they have always argued that how does this convert into numbers? How many people are you reaching, how can you be sure that you are reaching that number of people?

AVD : So then there will be a counter question as well that why government is spending millions of rupees for Digital India? Is government thinking that Digital India will become a successful tool to attract more foreign investment, then why not investing fraction of it and save millions of lives? That could be one option.

RB : Digital India is just about Swachh Bharat and making women more . . .

PD : Making women what?

RB : Pristine!

RDG: Okay, and what about – but do you think everyone understands how Planet Romeo or Grindr works? So I think there is also a level of literacy involved, wouldn't you say? I guess all of us know how . . .

RB : Yeah, most people have smart phones these days – like there are apps for women's safety, various NGOs launching apps for like safe zone marking, safe zones for women, so those are really effective I think, so if you could have something like that for sexual health . . .

AVD : Something like an app on sexual health?

RDG: Like a separate app do you mean?

RB : I think a separate app would be very good.

AVD : What I find is I mean like I'm talking about from a very grass roots level perspective. What I find is that when I scroll my Facebook page or when I scroll some apps, I tend to look at only those which have some 60 seconds or 90 seconds short videos. What I would like to see rather than reading for 6-7 minutes is something short and with audio-visuals. That affects a lot; that spreads the message like nothing else. Not much people are into reading, I might be or PD might be, but not all people into reading, but you have to reach out to those people because they do have sex and they could be vulnerable, they could be gay, straight whatever and their lives will be at risk or they might infect somebody else, you don't know. So apart from these long read-ups, which definitely people can do when they are free and if they are interested, you should have something short and crisp and have them out.

PB : And do you think which – with messages, what is the relationship between text and visuals? . . . I'm wondering if it's useful just to have visuals, sexual health photographic kind of message or story or – you know, I'm just thinking of some early kind of HIV intervention stuff where you had graphic novels, which were quite erotic, so there was an incentive to look at them anyway.

AVD : There was a Facebook page called Trans Health and I liked them and then they do have lot of short videos on trans individuals . . .

RDG: Is this India based?

AVD : No, I think this is US-based. So what was very interesting and startling to see was that the likes on their videos were around ranging from 1,000-4,000 and the viewers were like a few ten thousands. They had two videos back to back on how are transgender women become female from male, and so how does the genital surgery work out for women and for men. And they had some outstanding videos, very short but very outstanding. They started with this video showing a penis and all that stuff, and trust me the likes went to few 100,000s, and the viewers went towards a few millions. So one video could actually reach out to millions of people because of the message they had. I don't know how it works here, how it would work here . . .

PB : This was quite effective I think, it really had an impact.

AVD : Yes, it really had an impact. So people now know that they exist and then this is the way it works, so instead of asking people, they can always read and view it.

RDG: Can I ask one more question? All of you are looking at images and videos, so what makes you think that something that the website you're watching or the profile has the expertise to actually be giving that information, like what makes you trust that information coming from there, what is it that I can believe or that's not true? Because you know with anything online you always have that thing you never know.

AVD : It can be tricky, yes.

RDG: So personally, I just want to know personally for you what makes you decide.

RB : If I go through something on 'Varta', then definitely I can trust. Depends on people, face value, there is sometimes face value that can work, and if I'm looking at something that is random, definitely I go through various other websites to recheck.

PD : Can you elaborate on that face value - there must be something behind it. This example that you mentioned, if you trust any site, what would be behind that trust?

RB : See, first if I go through something like 'Varta', there are many stories I have gone through, I really like them because I found them very relatable. So I thought that somewhere I could see some parts of me in them, and I could make other people of the community read them. I mean there were real life stories, true stories and they were coming from the persons who have faced those issues, and faced those problems – or not just problems, because they are incidents coming from their own mouths, so that makes it more authentic, the style, the style of the blog, I took 'Varta' as an example. So it depends on how lucrative and attractive it is, and what style it is written in, how authentic it is, like the sources, the links given; there are certain websites that just have stories and they don't mention any links or back-ups or references from where they have got it. So this is more important I think.

PD : Have you all ever been through the NACO website or any

state government website?

RB : No.

AVD : No! (Laughter)

PB : That's a very emphatic no, why no?

RB : If you're talking about LGBTQI rights and sexual health of LGBTQI people, they are not at all – I don't think you would find anything useful on such sites, because for them we don't exist. So . . .

AVD : What I feel is like whatever is written on government websites, we individuals who are working on it know much more than what is written there. Second thing is like talking about the sites I actually would love to go ahead, like and watch videos, how do I go ahead and do it? I mean I have my own strategy, which is if my friends whom I can actually trust, if one of them like that page then yes, thumbs up, I would go ahead and do it; second is I would like to see what kind of stories they have. And a page which is talking about LGBT inclusion, if they talk about, if they have very sexist jokes, that is a big no-no for me; a page that talks about 'black lives matter', if they talk about something that is very homophobic, it's a big no-no for me. What I feel is like if a page talks about inclusion, you cannot make fun of some other identity. So that's one of the ways I like some pages, at the same time there are pages which have the links where they have found the stories, from where they made the short videos and yes, there are a few things I always keep in my mind. Sometimes it's pretty easy to be lost in the social media websites because of the names and because of the people. Couple of pages which talk about Palestine issues, I like that page and they have horrible stuff, they're talking about – I do support Palestine and all this stuff, but then I mean how could you talk about killing someone! I would not be a part of that kind of group. So it depends on what kind of pages you want. Like my dad – he keeps on liking those pages which talk about aliens, invaders and the like (laughter). So that interests him, but then he used to believe in all these stories, that was more frightening . . . but now with this process, he had a profile last year, it was a one year process. Yesterday he said something that I absolutely loved, there was a flower – so there is a sea animal, which looks like a flower and they claim that this flower was from the 'Ramayana' and 'Mahabharata' age and so Hindu and all this stuff. And my dad was like saying that 'Are these guys stupid, everybody knows that this is an animal!' So what I found is that what he was one year ago, and what he is now after a year, there are a lot of changes in him – so he learnt his lessons in a hard way, he kept on liking and sharing those pages and stories and then he got some backlash from my friends, from my mom, from me, how could you like this, this is not right. So yes, people learn from their mistakes, so that's one of the good ways of . . .

RB : I still like pages that have stories about ghosts!

PD : So if a ghost were to give a sexual health message, you would like it!

AVD : Maybe yes.

RB : Yes!

PB : It's interesting, what you're saying in relation to this is what kind of information do we seek - in a certain kind of way you're saying what PD earlier said . . . any kind of information on sexual health that comes from the State automatically one might regard with suspicion or just see it as not very well informed about these kind of issues. So where might the momentum come from, where might the impetus come from, is it just circumvent the State, or things that we were talking about we don't necessarily need - policies in place to support the kind of development of media platforms we do in the absence of policy, you know what I mean? If we have the State saying that we can work with you to develop the platform, then immediately you think that's going to alienate people, once you have the State stamp on it, it could actually become counter-productive. So where, who is going to fund it, where's it going to come from? . . . So I wonder where is the momentum and the funds and the energy going to come from, where should we apply pressure?

RDG: I mean your example (AVD) was so good, because this was like some individuals who just came together in Bangalore and spread messages about sexual health and safe sex, which is obviously relatively unfunded, you had no support – so I guess something that I found very impressive was how much more you trust the voice of the community and community pages rather than say government pages or anything – which also then kind of says so the expert might be community as such, that I much rather believe them than even if it's coming from a doctor whose got the government stamp.

RB : I have had this experience with doctors in government hospitals – like we were doing a film on transgender basic medical health care, so the doctor – I won't name the hospital – the doctor in the plastic surgery department did not know what is SRS. So you would not really trust people like that . . .

AVD : Government must do something, I mean that is a very idealistic situation, but then couple of days ago PD and I were talking that government officials - suppose PD has his own NGO, and he needs to have an audit system, so when government officials review the system, they might say, 'Oh, so you're working on sexual health or LGBT issues!' I mean you might get treated in some other way. You are then some of these alien beings. Government officials have absolutely no idea about these things and that makes our lives so hard. So even if I want to work and I understand that it is not feasible for the government to reach out to those people, so there is a scope of NGOs working towards it, but then how do you think a person would work? I mean I would like to have – at the end I would like to have a life which doesn't have much problems, but if I see so many problems, issues and suspicions from the government side, like the work I'm doing – I know the work is going to help people, but if the government official is not thinking like that, then I would not be very motivated, and after a couple of years I might say let's just leave it. I'm safe anyways so I don't need to work for people. So that motivation needs to come from the government – even if not money wise, but at least saying 'You know what, just go ahead what you're doing, you're doing great!' That message needs to come from the government. Unfortunately we don't have it.

RB : But there are ways, due to NGO interventions like sensitization programmes in various district hospitals – so I have heard stories where they are pretty much sensitized. Like in Srirampur Amitie' Trust is working, people over there are very much free about – they even have this man, woman, transgender – there is this separate column that you can fill up while getting admitted into a hospital – you don't have to fit into the other two things. So they are pretty sensitized, and they make you very comfortable. So there are NGOs which have made various hospitals and spaces like health related spaces very safe for people of alternate sexualities. At the same time things are going on, but you cannot just reach the top right now, the administration, because they are still very much blocked, I mean they put a deaf ear to such issues. But government officials at certain points of time, if they are human enough can really understand and they can give spaces for workshops and sensitization programmes. So there are places where these kinds of things are going on. I mean it's not totally hopeless. And also the digital platform, whatever little is there when I get anything I share it. So my college friends, university friends, school friends, my family, they see it and like it. These kind of individual efforts that you do, and what he said really works. And definitely there are NGOs, blogs and other things going on, films as well and sometimes advertisements are talking about such issues, not maybe health issues, but LGBT issues –

even if not in a very amplified way, but they are at least talking and speaking out. So these are certain milestones we can look up to, but . . .

AVD : No, but then there are steps taken by the NGOs, but the government must stop harassing them, how will they work? The government is actually harassing those NGOs in the name of so many things. I mean you cannot really work when you are being harassed. Can an individual be who they are and work towards . . .

RB : Yeah, trans women who work on such issues are often taken by police and they are asked to – they're raped, they're molested, so such issues are still there very much.

AVD : The funny thing is Amitie' Trust and the NGOs – they must establish a very good healthy relationship with the police and the government, which is not – I mean which is time consuming, because government may change in five years, so right now a political party is there and after five years there will be another. So once you do not have a strict policy regarding NGOs, so these things keep changing. For an example, right now the Government of India is absolutely regressive regarding these NGOs, funding and everything. So they keep questioning NGOs, they are actually cancelling their licence, all these things happening right now. So how do you think the NGOs will be working? And I'm okay with cancelling the licence of the NGOs, but the government should pick up that work where the void has been created. What essentially we started doing, people like PD and all, started doing in 2004, and we progressed so much till 2014. Right now actually we're going back. So this space has been taken, snatched away by the government because they are thinking that if we talk about sexual health then you are actually speaking against the government.

RB : The government is right now very non-secular, patriarchal and everything. They really don't talk about anything with pictures - I don't think they are very sensitive to the word sex . . . And they have passed this NALSA verdict, which is very freaky, like there is no – I mean they are denying the definition and the whole struggle of transgender people. The very definition that they have mentioned in the act is very disturbing.

RDG: Sure, and there is this consultation meeting that's going to happen soon.

RB : There is this one consultation that has happened, they have clarified that who is a trans woman – they have said neither male nor female, but male and female are not gender terms. They are biological sex, so they're saying neither male, nor female.

RDG: Before we move on to anything, I know we're running out of time, so I've got one final question, unless PB you have something more to say, to just kind of wrap up. And this is again going to be quite a subjective one. So I'm going to ask you – if you could say that you think making online sexual health outreach would be much more - something that you would – what would you like to see in online sexual health outreach, what would make you think right that's a good way to go, I would actually recommend that, or I would get that information?

RB : For me I think that there are various links, sponsored links, like when you scroll down your Facebook page, you see various links on films happenings, sponsored links, so they talk about various social acts like there was this very cute and lively entertaining video on women, freedom of women - they have the right to work and they have the right to choose their profession, there was this very interesting video on that – so there are certain links . . . I don't remember the name . . . it was in June, a three minutes video . . . I want to see such videos on sexual health. And I think that is very, very – that attracts people . . . there are millions of videos going where you can see links, Youtube links or links of other websites. So I think there need to be more videos on gender, sexuality and sexual health.

And that won't be very raw, like just educational videos won't do, it would need to be packaged more, more palatable.

AVD : Yeah, it should be crisp and small . . .

RB : And with stories.

AVD : Yeah, I mean like I'm being a queer person I would not want always like to see gay, gay – trans, trans, rather I would like to see a world where everything is included. So a page which talks about sexual health, irrespective of their gender identity, sexual orientation – this is something I would like to see which doesn't happen, which is not happening right now, and a very short and crisp message through audio-visual is great. Yes, the link has to be there where people can read up more.

RB : That is why I talked about corporates because they fund on such videos and then they are open to it. I have gone to various corporates and they think that it's okay, as long as it caters to certain products or brands of them . . . the corporates are evolving and their policies are evolving and they are open to talking about queer issues. They are like - TCS wanted to be a part of the pride walk, but the pride walk did not want corporate involvement. But they are open to it.

AVD : I'll just give an example that just came to my mind. Couple of months ago I saw an advertisement of Dove, Dove soap – talks about diversity of women. The moment you talk about women, care, beauty, all those soaps, all those so called fairness creams, they only portray a fair woman. What Dove did was absolutely amazing, in that 59 seconds of video, they picked up Indians of different colours - the moment you think about an Indian person you see an Indian lady wearing a saree with a bindi and long hair, which is not true! I mean like we have, we are more diverse than anyone else – and the fact that we completely exclude people from ethnic looks, Asian looking people who live in our North-East part of India, as if they are not a part of India. So what Dove did was wonderful, they picked up at least 1,000 women with different colours, different hair styles, and different dressing styles. It was a wonderful video, and the message, of course, they wanted to advertise their own product, but the message of inclusiveness which they had was wonderful.

RB : So if they have this, if they can advertise their product, they will be open to it.

AVD : Open to all, I mean they're not only open for young, long haired, with bindi, saree wearing, slim, fair women.

RDG: Brilliant! So that's great, it was really great talking to both of you, I think we got lots of information and it also challenged us as well to think about things that we were not thinking about. So thanks a lot!

BIBLIOGRAPHY

Alexander, J. and Losh, E. (2010). 'A Youtube of one's own: Coming out videos as rhetorical action', in C. Pullen and M. Cooper (eds.). *LGBT identity and Online New Media.* Oxon: Routledge, 37-50

Arondekar, A. (2009). *For the Record: On Sexuality and the Colonial Archive.* Durham: Duke University Press.

Ballhatchet, K. (1980). *Race, Sex and Class during the British Raj.* London: Palgrave Macmillan.

Bachcheta, P. (1999). 'When the (Hindu) nation exiles its queers', *Social Text*, 61: 141-166.

Bachcheta, P. (2007). 'Rescaling transnational queerdom: Lesbian and lesbian identitary positionalities in Delhi in the 1980's.' in N. Menon (ed.). *Sexualities.* New Delhi: Women Unlimited, 103-127.

Banerjea, N. (2014). 'Critical urban collaborative ethnographies: Articulating community with Sappho for equality in Kolkata, India.' *Gender, Place and Culture: A Journal of Feminist Geography* (Online First).

Bhaskaran, S. (2002). 'The politics of penetration: Section 377 and the Indian penal code', in Ruth Vanita (ed). *Queering India: Same Sex Love and Eroticism in Indian Culture and Society*, London: Routledge, 15-29.

Bhaskaran, S. (2004). *Made in India.* New York: Palgrave Macmillan.

Boyce, P. (2006). 'Moral ambivalence and irregular practices: Contextualizing male-to-male sexualities in Calcutta/India'. *Feminist Review*, 83 (1). 79-98.

Boyce, P. (2007). '(Dis)locating men who have sex with men in Calcutta: Subject, space and perception,' in B. Bose and S. Bhattacharyya (eds.). *The Phobic and the Erotic: The Politics of Sexualities in Contemporary India*. Kolkata: Seagull.

Boyce, P. (2014). 'Desirable rights: Same-sex sexual subjectivities, socio-economic transformations, global flows and boundaries in India and beyond'. *Culture, Health & Sexuality: An International Journal for Research, Intervention and Care*, 16 (10): 1201-1215.

Butler, J. (1999). *Gender Trouble: Feminism and Subversion of Identity*. London: Routledge.

Burgess, J. and Green, J. (2009). *Youtube*. Cambridge: Polity.

Bryman, A. (2008). 'Of methods and methodology', *Qualitative Research in Organizations and Management: An International Journal*, 3(2): 159-168.

Campbell, C. and Cornish, F. (2010). 'Towards a fourth generation of approaches to HIV and AIDS management: Creating contexts for effective community mobilisation. *AIDS Care*, 22(1): 1569-1579.

Campbell, J.E. (2004), *Getting it on Online: Cyberspace, Gay Male Sexuality and Embodied Identity*. New York: Harrington Park Press.

Chakrapani, V., Newman, P. and Shunmugam, M. (2008). 'Secondary HIV prevention among *Kothi* identified MSM in Chennai, India'. *Culture, Health and Sexuality*, 10(4): 313-327.

Clift, J. (2010). 'Health information, STDs, and the internet: Implications for gay men', in C. Pullen and M. Cooper (eds.). *LGBT Identity and Online New Media* (pp. 258-270). London/New York: Routledge.

Cottle, S. and Lester, L. (2011). 'Transnational protests and the media: An introduction', in Cottle, S. and Lester, L. (eds.). *Transnational Protests and the Media*. Oxford: Peter Lang, pp. 3-16.

Counsel Club (2002). *A Self-Help Story*. Humjinsi: A Resource Book on Lesbian, Gay and Bisexual Rights in India, India Centre for Human Rights and Law. Also the *Dateline* from the same resource book.

Creswell, J.W. (2014). *Research Design: Qualitative, Quantitative and Mixed Methods Approach*. London: Sage.

Gosine, A. (2009). 'Monster, womb, MSM: The work of sex in international development'. *Development*, 52(1): 25-33.

Das, A. and Dhall, P. (2013). *Culture and Issues of Rights to the Eyes of the Indians with 'Other' Self-identities of Sexuality and Gender.* Human Rights and the Third World – Issues and Discourses, Lexington Books.

Dasgupta, R.K. (2012). 'Digital media and the internet for HIV prevention, capacity building and advocacy among gay, other men who have sex with men (MSM) and transgenders: Perspectives from Kolkata, India.' *Digital Culture and Education*, 4(1): 88-109.

Dasgupta, R.K. (2014). 'Parties, advocacy and activism: Interrogating community and class in digital queer India', in Christopher Pullen (ed.). *Queer Youth and Media Cultures.* Basingstoke: Palgrave Macmillan, 265-277.

Dasgupta, R.K. (2015). 'Dissident citizenship: Articulating belonging, dissidence and queerness on cyberspace', *South Asian Review*, 35(3): 203-223.

Dasgupta, R.K. (2016). 'Queering virtual intimacies in contemporary India', in B. Scherer (ed.). *Queer/Variable Bodies, Ethics and Glocal Struggles.* Oxford/New York: Peter Lang, 197-213.

Dasgupta, R.K. (2017). *Digital Queer Cultures in India: Politics, Intimacies and Belonging.* London: Routledge.

Dave, N. (2012). *Queer Activism in India: An Anthropology in Ethics.* Durham: Duke UP.

Dhall, P. and Boyce, P. (2015). *Livelihood, Exclusion and Opportunity: Socioeconomic Welfare among Gender and Sexuality Non-normative People in India.* IDS Evidence Report 106. Sussex: Institute of Development Studies.

Dhall, P. (2005). 'Solitary Cruiser', in A. Narrain and G. Bhan (eds.). *Because I have a Voice: Queer Politics in India.* Delhi: Yoda Press, 115-142.

Driver, S. (2005). 'Out, creative and questioning: Reflexive self representations in queer youth homepages.' *Canadian Woman Studies*, 24(2-3), 111-116.

Drushel, B. (2010). 'Virtually supportive: Self disclosure of minority sexualities through online social networking sites', in C. Pullen and M. Cooper (eds). *LGBT Identity and Online New Media*. Oxon: Routledge, 62-74.

Gajjala, R. and Mitra, R. (2008). 'Queer blogging in Indian digital diasporas: A dialogic encounter', *Journal of Communication Inquiry*, 32(4), 400-423.

Gupta, A. (2005). 'Englishpur ki Kothi: Class dynamics in the queer movement in India', in A. Narrain and G. Bhan (eds). *Because I have a Voice: Queer Politics in India* (pp. 123-142). Delhi: Yoda Press.

Gutierrez, J., McPherson, S., Fakoya, A., Matheou, A. and Bertozzi, S. (2010). 'Community-based prevention leads to an increase in condom use and a reduction in sexually transmitted infections (STIs) among men who have sex with men (MSM) and female sex workers (FSW): The Frontiers Prevention Project (FPP) evaluation results. *BMC Public Health*, 10(497): 1-12.

Hazra, A., Roy, S., Pattanayak, B.B., Dhall, P., Mohanty, M., Pyne, S., Ramakrishnan, L. and Raghavan, S.S. (2012). *Collaborative Advocacy Route to Health Equity for PLHIV and Sexual Minorities*, poster presentation at AIDS 2012, Washington DC, USA.

Hazra, A. and Ghosh, S. (2016). *Pehchan Conundrum*. Varta, May 2016.

Hine, C. (2015). *Ethnography for the Internet: Embedded, Embodied and Everyday*. London: Bloomsbury.

Hutchby, I. (2001). 'Technologies, Texts and Affordances'. *Sociology*, 35(2): 441–456.

Jenkins, H. (2009). *Convergence Culture: Where Old and New Media Collide*. New York: New York University Press.

Joseph, S. (2005). *Social Work Practice and Men Who Have Sex with Men*, Sage Publications.

Joseph, S. and Dhall, P. (2000). *Les-Bi-Gay Voices from India – No Silence Please, We're Indians*. Different Rainbows, Gay Men's Press.

Kumar, S. (1998). *Model for Sexual Health Found in India's West Bengal*. The Lancet, 1998, Jan 3; 351(9095): 46.

Landers, S., Pickett, J., Rennie, L. and Wakefield, S. (2011). Community perspectives on developing a sexual health agenda for gay and bisexual men', *AIDS and Behavior*, 15(1), Supplement: 101-106.

Macmaster, S., Aquino, R. and Vail, K. (2003). 'Providing HIV education and outreach via internet chat rooms to men who have sex with men', *Journal of Human Behavior in the Social Environment*, 8: 2-3, 145-151.

Markham, A.N. (2016, in press). 'Ethnography in the digital era: From fields to flow, descriptions to interventions', in Denzin, N. and Lincoln, Y. (eds.). *The Sage Handbook of Qualitative Research*, 5th Edition. Thousand Oaks, CA: Sage.

McGlotten, S. (2007). 'Virtual intimacies: Love, addiction, and identity @ The Matrix', in K. O'Riordan and D. Phillips (eds.). *Queer Online: Media, Technology and Society*. New York: Peter Lang, 123-137.

McGlotten, S. (2013). *Virtual Intimacies: Media, Affect and Queer Sociality*. Albany: SUNY Press.

Mclelland, M. (2002). 'Virtual ethnography: Using the internet to study gay culture in Japan'. *Sexualities*, 5(4): 387-406.

McRobbie, A. (2010). 'Reflections on feminism, immaterial labour, and the post fordist regime'. *New Formations*, 60-76.

Mishra, M. (2016). *Keeping Up the Momentum on AIDS*, India HIV/AIDS Alliance, 2014: http://www.allianceindia.org/keeping-momentum-aids/ (last accessed December 7, 2016).

Mowlabocus, S. (2008). 'Revisiting old haunts through new technologies: Public (homo)sexual cultures in cyberspace'. *International Journal of Cultural Studies*, 11(4): 419-439.

Mowlabocus, S. (2010). *Gaydar Culture: Gay Men, Technology and Embodiment in the Digital Age*. Farnham/Burlington: Ashgate.

Mowlabocus, S. Harbottle, J, Dasgupta, R.K. and Haslop, C. (2014). 'Reaching out online: Digital literacy and the uses of social media in health promotion'. *Working Papers of the Communities & Culture Network*, Vol. 3 (April 2014).

Mowlabocus, S., Harbottle, J., Tooke, B., Haslop, C. and Dasgupta R.K. (2015). 'Because even the placement of a comma might be important: Expertise, embodiment and social capital in online sexual health promotion'. *Convergence: The International Journal of Research into New Media Technologies*, 21(3): 375-387.

Mowlabocus, S., Haslop, C. and Dasgupta, R.K. (2016). 'From scene to screen: The challenges and opportunities of commercial digital platforms for HIV community outreach'. *Social Media and Society*, 2(4): 1-8.

MSMGF Report (2010). Retrieved 05 March 2012, from http://www.msmgf.org/files/msmgf/About_Us/MSMGF_Quarterly_Report_10_June_2010.pdf

NACO (2002). *National Baseline High Risk and Bridge Population Behavioural Surveillance Survey, 2002.*

NACO (2009). *NACO Report.* New Delhi: Department of AIDS Control, Ministry of Health and Family Welfare, Government of India.

NACO (2014). *NACO Report.* New Delhi: Department of AIDS Control, Ministry of Health and Family Welfare, Government of India.

Narrain, A. (2004). *Queer: Despised Sexuality, Law and Social Change.* Bangalore: Books for Change.

NACO (2016). *National AIDS Control Program – Phase IV Mid-Term Appraisal – HIV Prevention among Key and Vulnerable Populations (Targeted Interventions).*

Palm Avenue Integration Society (2002). *Network East '02: A Conference on Creative Communication – The Key to Better Sexual Health, Calcutta, January 25-27, 2002.*

Pedrana, A. et al. (2013). 'Queer as F**k: Reaching and engaging gay men in sexual health promotion through social networking sites'. *Journal of Medical Internet Research,* 15(2). Available at: http://www.jmir.org/2013/2/e25/

Pravartak (1996). *Radio Gay Gay!* and other stories in the Cityscope column of Pravartak, July-December 1996.

Ramakrishnan, L. (nd). ICTs and the fight against HIV and AIDS in India. *Oneworld.Net.* Retrieved February 21, 2012, from http://uk.oneworld.net/article/view/108250/1/1912?PrintableVersion=enabled

Ramakrishnan, L. (2007). 'Putting the B back in LGBT: Bisexuality, queer politics and HIV and AIDS discourse', in B. Bose and S.

Bhattacharya (eds.). *The Phobic and the Erotic* (pp. 291-300). Kolkata: Seagull.

Reddy G. (2005). *With Respect to Sex – Negotiating Hijra Identity in South India*, University of Chicago Press.

Rosser, B.R. et al. 'The future of internet-based HIV prevention: A report on key findings from the men's internet (MINTS-I, II) sex studies'. *AIDS and Behavior,* 15(1) Supplement: 91-100.

Roy, S. (2003). 'From khush list to gay Bombay: Virtual webs of real people', in C. Berry, F. Martin and A. Yue (eds.). *Mobile Cultures: New Media in Queer Asia*. Durham: Duke UP, 180-200.

SAATHII (2011). *Policy Brief: Health Policies and Sexual and Reproductive Health Needs of People Living with HIV and Sexual Minorities in Orissa and West Bengal*, SAATHII, Interact WorldWide, DFID.

Sahani, P. (2008*). Gay Bombay: Globalisation, Love and (Be)longing in Contemporary India*. New Delhi: Sage.

Sandelowski, M. (2004). 'Using qualitative research'. *Qualitative Health Research,* 14(10): 1366-1386.

Shaw, D. (1997). 'Gay men and computer communication', in S. Jones (ed.). *Virtual Culture: Identity and Communication in Cybersociety* (pp. 133-145). New Delhi/Thousand Oaks/London: Sage.

Shrivastava, S. (ed.) (2005). *Sexual Sites, Seminal Attitudes, Sexualities, Masculinities and Culture in South Asia*. New Delhi/London: Sage.

Silveira, A. (2010). 'Giving a queer account of the self and culture'. *Canon Magazine*. Retrieved February 12, 2012 from www.canonmagazine.org/spring10/silveira.html

Singh, G. and Walsh, C.S. (2012). *Building the HIVe: Disrupting Biomedical HIV/AIDS Research with Gay Men, Other MSM and Transgenders*. AERA 2012.

Singh, P. (2016). *Far from a Miniscule Minority: The Online Worlds of Indian Queer Men,* Queer Potli: Memories, imaginations and re-imaginations of urban queer spaces in India, Ed. Pawan Dhall, Queer Ink.

Singh, S., Dasgupta, S., Pattankar, P. and Sinha, M. (2012). *A People Stronger: The Collectivization of MSM and TG Groups in India*, UNDP, Sage Publications.

Terranova, T. (2004). *Network Culture: Politics for the Information Age*, London, Pluto Press.

Vanita, R. and Kidwai, S. (eds.) (2000). *Same Sex Love in India: Readings in Indian Literature*. New York: Palgrave Macmillan.

Vanita, R. (ed) (2002). *Queering India: Same Sex Love and Eroticism in Indian Culture and Society*. London: Routledge.

Waites, M. (2010). 'Human rights, sexual orientation and the generation of childhoods: Analysing the partial decriminalisation of "unnatural offences" in India.' *International Journal of Human Rights,* 14(6), pp. 971–93.

Wakeford, N. (1997). 'Cyberqueer', in A. Medhurst and S. Munt (eds.). *Lesbian and Gay Studies: A Critical Introduction* (pp. 20-38). London: Cassell.

Walsh, C.S. (2008). 'Producing animations to educate MSM and MSW to fashion safe sex practices and address low perceptions of personal risk', in: *IADIS Multi Conference on Computer Science and Information Systems*, 22-24 July 2008, Amsterdam, The Netherlands.

Walsh, C.S., Lasky, B. and Morrish, W. (2011). 'Building local capacity to protect public health and promote social justice through online peer education', in *IADIS International Conference e-Democracy, Equity and Social Justice 2011*, part of the IADIS Multi Conference on Computer Science and Information Systems 2011, 20-22 July 2011, Rome, Italy.

Welfare, W.S. and Lighton, L. (2011). 'Mapping of sexual health promotion in North West England, 2008'. *Public Health,* 125: 101-105.

Young, S.D. and Jaganathan, D. (2013). 'Feasibility of using social networking technologies for health research among men who have sex with men: A mixed methods study'. *American Journal of Men's Health*, XX(X): 1-9.